PORTFOLIO

MANAGEMENT REWIRED

Charles S. Jacobs is the managing partner of 180 Partners and an adviser to Fortune 500 companies. He was also the founder of the Amherst Consulting Group and has worked in Europe, Asia, and the United States. His clients include Exxon-Mobil, Verizon, Bristol-Myers Squibb, and more than fifty of the world's largest corporations. An active speaker and lecturer, he lives in Boston.

MANAGEMENT REWIRED

Why Feedback Doesn't Work

and Other Surprising Lessons

from the Latest Brain Science

CHARLES S. JACOBS

PORTFOLIO

PORTFOLIO

Published by the Penguin Group

Penguin Group (USA) Inc., 375 Hudson Street, New York, New York 10014, U.S.A.
Penguin Group (Canada), 90 Eglinton Avenue East, Suite 700, Toronto,
Ontario, Canada M4P 2Y3 (a division of Pearson Penguin Canada Inc.)
Penguin Books Ltd, 80 Strand, London WC2R 0RL, England
Penguin Ireland, 25 St Stephen's Green, Dublin 2, Ireland (a division of Penguin Books Ltd)
Penguin Group (Australia), 250 Camberwell Road, Camberwell, Victoria 3124, Australia
(a division of Pearson Australia Group Pty Ltd)
Penguin Books India Pvt Ltd, 11 Community Centre, Panchsheel Park,
New Delhi – 110 017, India
Penguin Group (NZ), 67 Apollo Drive, Rosedale, North Shore 0632, New Zealand
(a division of Pearson New Zealand Ltd)
Penguin Books (South Africa) (Pty) Ltd, 24 Sturdee Avenue, Rosebank,
Johannesburg 2196, South Africa

Penguin Books Ltd, Registered Offices:
80 Strand, London WC2R 0RL, England

First published in the United States of America by Portfolio,
a member of Penguin Group (USA) Inc. 2009
This paperback edition with a new preface published 2010

1 3 5 7 9 10 8 6 4 2

THE LIBRARY OF CONGRESS HAS CATALOGED THE HARDCOVER EDITION AS FOLLOWS:
Jacobs, Charles S.
Management rewired : why feedback doesn't work and other surprising
lessons from the latest brain science / Charles S. Jacobs.
p. cm.
Includes bibliographical references and index.
ISBN 978-1-59184-262-0 (hc.)
ISBN 978-1-59184-337-5 (pbk.)
1. Psychology, Industrial.   2. Interpersonal relations—Psychological aspects.
3. Personnel management—Psychological aspects.   4. Organizational behavior.
5. Management.   I. Title.
HF5548.8.J24 2009
658.001'9—dc22   2009001724

Printed in the United States of America
Set in Scala   •   Designed by Jaime Putorti

To Jonas, the teacher who taught me the value of ideas,
and to my daughters, Julia and Emma,
who will only listen to stories

CONTENTS

PREFACE TO THE PAPERBACK EDITION

A preface is an opportunity to set expectations and shape how readers will view what's to come. It's a chance to focus attention on what's most significant about the work and to frame how it should be interpreted. There would be little reason for a preface if we all saw things the same way. But according to the latest scientific research, we don't.

Out of all the data bombarding our senses, we become conscious of only a small sample, and how we make sense of it is determined by the unique way our brains are wired. Although it may seem that we're just recording our impressions of the world, *f*MRI scans of the brain show that our perceptions are a function of our feelings, desires, and memories. Rather than video cameras, our minds operate more like storytellers, spinning our own unique version of events.

Just as authors can never be sure their work will be read as they intend, so too can we never be sure that our words and actions will be read by others as we intend. Nor can we be certain that our interpretation of what others mean is accurate. In fact, we can't even be certain that we know what we mean, for not only is the world different than we believe, so is the way we think about it.

Although humans are assumed to be rational beings pursuing self-interest, experiments have shown that our decisions are made unconsciously, and that they are frequently anything but reasonable. Actions based on the belief that people are rational have a distressing tendency to produce the opposite of what we want.

But identifying the problems with the way we currently reason doesn't mean we should abandon it. In light of the recent discoveries, the role of conscious reasoning becomes even more important. It enables us to manage those unconscious processes that drive our decisions and actions, and to account for the perceptions of others. We just need to make some simple adjustments to the way we think.

When we shift our view of the world to incorporate our new understanding of how our minds work, we gain a greater appreciation of what drives our thinking and behavior, as well as that of others. We then know what actions we need to take to be more effective, no matter how unreasonable they may first appear. In business, the benefits go right to the bottom line. We become better at satisfying our customers, thwarting our competitors, and inspiring our employees. Our efforts are more focused and our organizations more efficient.

The insights we're gaining from brain science are nothing short of fantastic. We're learning that the world we live in is more mental than physical, that it's created anew every moment, and that it can be transformed by an idea. Even so, this is as pragmatic a book as can be. It is about how to use the latest discoveries to be more effective in this world. It explains why so many of the management practices we take for granted fail and it offers straightforward ways to improve both business performance and our quality of work life.

Ultimately, what brain science teaches us about management

just makes sense. It complements the growing body of research linking specific practices to improvements in performance, and it dovetails with our society's deepest values, our beliefs about how people should be treated in a just and fair world, and our own aspirations. The ends may not be new, but now we have a better understanding of the means to achieve them.

INTRODUCTION

It turns out that most of what we thought we knew about management is probably wrong. New research shows that our emotions lead to better business decisions than our logic. Positive and negative feedback not only don't improve performance, they tend to make it worse. The quantifiable objectives that are a critical part of our strategic plans cause us to focus on the short term at the expense of the long term. Many of the management practices we've taken for granted are not only ineffective, they actually produce the opposite of what we intend.

At the same time, new approaches that have been proven to produce superior performance can't help but strike us as unreasonable. It's been demonstrated that smaller rewards tend to be more motivational than larger ones, that being competitive is often the best way to encourage cooperation, and that the managers who produce the best results are the ones who do the least managing.

The latest developments in brain science are teaching us a better way to manage, but they also challenge our common sense. Using functional magnetic resonance imaging, or the *f*MRI as it's known in the field, scientists are now able to watch the brain at work, and what they're learning is mind-boggling. Not only have they located the areas of the brain that are responsible for our emotions, our reason, and even our moral character; they've also discovered what makes us empathetic, able to learn, and take pleasure in our work. They've even figured out why teenagers drive their parents so crazy.

But perhaps the most surprising discovery has come from mapping the path information travels from our sense organs to our awareness of the world we live in. Not only are the perceptual areas of the brain involved, so are the areas responsible for our memories, our feelings, our beliefs, and our aspirations. Our minds aren't objectively recording our experience of the world; they're creating it, and that creation is influenced by everything else going on in the brain. Each of us lives in a mental world of our own making.

This isn't just some abstract, philosophical issue. It has enormous practical ramifications for how we live and work. The world we know is only what we think it to be, and we can't assume other people will think the same way we do. In fact, we know they won't. Since our customers, employees, peers, and bosses all see things differently than we do, the way we act toward them doesn't necessarily produce the results we expect or want.

While most of us accept that others see the world differently than we do, we trust in our objective, logical reasoning to resolve conflicting perceptions. But the *f*MRI also shows us that objective reasoning has nothing to do with the way we solve problems, make decisions, and plan for the future. At best, logic is just a way to justify conclusions we have already reached unconsciously.

This new understanding of how the mind works needs to be incorporated into all of our thinking about business. The resulting management practices may seem illogical, but they'll produce better performance. Our organizations will be more focused and efficient, and our strategies more effective at creating a sustainable advantage. We'll also be able to meaningfully transform businesses rapidly, and our leadership will bring out the best in people. The improvement in the bottom line will not just be incremental, but a quantum leap.

Any manager who's been around for a while has heard bold claims like this before only to end up disappointed by the latest and greatest initiative that doesn't live up to its promise. But brain science's transformation of management isn't just about another new technique or model. It's about shifting our paradigm to incorporate the hard data of science and fundamentally changing the way we think about business. When we do, we're able to gain access to an integrated set of management practices that really do deliver on the promise of superior performance.

With such enormous potential, why hasn't there been more interest in applying the insights of brain science to management? The reason is that our logical thinking excels at dividing things up and categorizing them. While this enables us to organize vast amounts of knowledge, it also separates what we know into specialties with their own unique language and ways of thinking. It's a daunting task for a layperson to come to grips with the complex Latinate terms of neuroscience. Businesspeople and brain scientists living in their own worlds have difficulty communicating and appreciating one another's concerns.

But this problem is an opportunity for those in business who are able to bridge the gap. It immediately gives them a leg up on the competitors who don't appreciate how the findings of brain science can be applied to their businesses. Nor is the application difficult once the implications of the basic discoveries are understood. There are no complicated algorithms or complex processes to master. With a just subtle shift of perspective it becomes clear what approaches don't work and how to generate ones that do. All you need to do is use the mind the way we now know it naturally works.

This book explains what the latest discoveries mean and how they transform our understanding of the way people. think and behave. For each key area of management, from strategy to leadership, it shows the limitations of our current practices and details the new, often counterintuitive approaches that are in line with how the mind actually works. It then demonstrates specifically what managers can do in each area to improve the performance of their businesses. Implementing these new approaches is surprisingly easy. The biggest challenge is for managers to stop doing most of what they're doing now.

While the goal is a healthier bottom line, management based on the insights of brain science brings other benefits as well. When a manager's actions aren't producing the opposite of what they intend, management becomes easier, less stressful, and more fun. When people are managed in a way that encourages their natural inclinations, they find their work more rewarding. It's good for the business, for the manager, and for the people.

Leaving aside the practical benefits, the latest discoveries of brain science are fascinating in their own right, and the path we'll travel in applying them to business is full of interesting twists and turns. Along the way, we'll meet a hero who taught the world the best strategists are consummate liars. We'll watch a student whose inability to understand an idea has made the jobs of managers so frustrating. We'll see children whose IQs rise dramatically only because their teacher was deceived into believing they would, and a dolphin that learns to shift paradigms. While it's a unique and at times strange story, the end point is the best way to quickly improve business results.

I am out in the corporate world every day, and I see intelligent, well-meaning managers imprisoned by the conventional wisdom and frustrated by their inability to get an organization of people to do what they need them to do. I watch as the endless parade of new corporate initiatives produce disappointing results. At the same time, I know from experience that virtually every company can be more successful and that the success can be achieved far more easily and far more quickly than most believe is possible.

Understanding the recent discoveries of neuroscience can't help but change the way people think, and when their application to business is demonstrated, managers realize ways to improve performance that, while often counterintuitive, produce better results with less effort. With a perspective informed by science and a set of tools proven effective in the business world, managers will know what they need to do, not just for the bottom line, but for the people whose efforts are measured by that bottom line.

ONE

BRAIN SCIENCE

We assume that our minds, to a greater or lesser extent, faithfully record our experience of the world. While we'll acknowledge that our view of individual events is subjective, we don't question for a minute that there is a world that exists independently of us. In fact, one of the basic assumptions of science is that we can have objective knowledge of the world and everything that's in it.

But according to the latest research in neuroscience, such knowledge is impossible. The only world we can know is the mental one produced by the firing of our neurons, and it is purely subjective. While information from our senses may be input, it is assembled, edited, and assigned significance according to everything else going on in the brain. We don't record our experience of the world as much as we create it. Neuroscience doesn't deny that there's a world out there, it simply says that all we can know is our *version* of it.

Scientists call these different versions *paradigms*, and they view them as frameworks for making sense of our experience. The historian of science Thomas Kuhn saw the swapping of one paradigm for another as a kind of cognitive revolution, causing not just an incremental increase in the knowledge we have, but a quantum leap to a different, more comprehensive kind of knowledge. Because paradigms drive the way we think and the way we act, it's difficult to overestimate the far-reaching effects of embracing a new one.

The classic example is the transformation of our view of the universe during the Renaissance. Until the sixteenth century, both the conventional wisdom and science held that the earth was at the center, and the sun, planets, and stars revolved around it. This earth-centric paradigm was already beginning to break down because the planets weren't always where it predicted them to be. Epicycles were added to orbits, and numerous other adjustments were made to account for the deviations. The paradigm grew increasingly complex, but it still didn't fit the facts.

Then Copernicus realized that the conventional wisdom had it inside out. The planets didn't revolve around the earth; rather, the earth and the other planets revolved around the sun. This new, greatly simplified paradigm was a much better fit with the observable data.

The discoveries of neuroscience have shifted the paradigm of how the mind works, and as a result, they are challenging our beliefs about the very nature of the world we know and how best to think about it. When it comes to business, the effect is nothing short of revolutionary. This isn't just about making use of a new management technique, model, or practice. The latest research goes right at the way we think about management, highlighting fundamental flaws in our current approaches and offering in their place others that challenge everything we take for granted about how best to manage.

THE MATTER OF MIND

The appearance of the brain doesn't offer us many clues about what it does. When we open up the skull and look at the brain, all we see is a grayish mass with a jello-like consistency. There is nothing we can observe to indicate the organ's function or purpose or suggest that this three pounds of flesh is the most complex system on the planet. When Aristotle looked at the brain, it seemed to him to be some sort of radiator to cool the blood. He thought the heart was the seat of the mind.

As scientists began studying the brain, they were able to make out different structures. By correlating structural damage caused by disease or injury with the loss of mental functions, they created maps identifying where various mental faculties were believed to reside. These maps have grown quite complex over time, and making sense of them is complicated by the Latin terms used to identify the different structures and their locations. It also doesn't help that not all neuroscientists slice and dice the brain in the same way.

But even a quick overview of the anatomy of the brain provides some interesting clues to how our minds work. There are specific areas dedicated to the processing of sense data, the maintenance of attention, the storing and recall of memory, and the higher-order thought that we believe is unique to humans and a few other primates. Our brains register our experience of the external world, select aspects of it to attend to, perform operations on these aspects, and save the results in memory, all not unlike what a computer is capable of.

But very much unlike a computer, an area of the brain known as the amygdala generates feelings that can direct, color, and transform the brain's cognitive operations. Perhaps we could think of it as a laptop with an attitude that changes moment to moment, but even that doesn't quite capture it. For the way the brain works determines both who we are and what kind of world we operate in, and neither of these two is anything at all like the way we thought them to be. This becomes strikingly clear when we look at how we make decisions.

THE HEART HAS REASONS

The way we think in the business world is supposed to be objective and logical. We quantify everything we can and guard against any emotions that might hijack our reasoning. While we often acknowledge gut feelings, no manager interested in continuing employment would make a serious financial decision without having the numbers and the logic to back it up. But according to the neurologist Antonio Damasio, the seat of our conscious thought, the prefrontal cortex, has a reciprocal connection with the emotion-generating amygdala, ensuring that we don't make our decisions with objective logic, despite our belief that we do. In fact, he conducted an ingenious experiment proving that if we did, we'd make bad decisions.

A subject is given $2,000 of play money to make wagers on the results of turning over a card from one of four decks labeled A, B, C, and D. The subject is not told how long the game will last, but each card will either result in earning or losing money. The given payoffs or costs are disclosed only after the turn of the card. The cards in decks A and B either win $100 or lose as much as $1,250. Those in decks B and C pay $50, but lose only up to $100.

Normal players sample all four decks and early on show an initial preference for A and B and their larger payoffs. After a while, however, they shift to C and D, apparently recognizing the high risk of the A and B decks. However, patients with lesions in the ventromedial area of the prefrontal cortex showed a sustained preference for the high risk A and B decks, even as their losses bankrupted them.

Damasio hypothesizes that the patients with the lesions had lost the ability to anticipate and plan for the future. Instead, they were ruled by the now. This ability to plan for the future has to do with what Damasio calls somatic markers. After trial and error, normal patients learned to associate a selection from decks A and B with a *feeling* of "badness." This feeling biased them away from choosing those two decks. The ventromedial area is, as you might expect, connected to the amygdala.

In a follow-up experiment, the game was played with subjects who had their skin conductive response measured, as in a lie detector test. Prior to the selection of the deck, normal patients experienced an increase in the magnitude of the response, and the magnitude continued to grow as the game continued. In other words, the prediction of "badness" from decks A and B was made unconsciously *before* the conscious decision of which deck to select was made. Emotions drove the prediction.

These findings explain how we actually make decisions. Our past experiences carry an emotional charge that is encoded in memories. When we encounter a situation similar enough to summon up those past experiences, along with their associated emotions, our prospective choices are marked by those emotions. We then are motivated to choose the ones that are "good" versus the ones that are "bad." This means that the more we attempt to strip out feelings and create an objective decision-making process, the more we lose access to what we have learned from past experiences.

Damasio's experiment raises questions about how much "I" am really in control. While the conventional wisdom holds that I consciously solve problems and make decisions, the results of the experiment suggest otherwise: I become aware of the solution or the decision when it has already been arrived at through processes that are not conscious. Perhaps even more counterintuitive is that emotions, not logic, drive the decision-making process. The ideal of decision making in the corporate world—rigorous objectivity—virtually ensures the loss of what's been learned through experience. It appears that it isn't the pressure from Wall Street for quarterly results that prevents an adequate long-term perspective, but our preference for supposedly objective thinking.

The results of Damasio's experiment make it clear that we're not reasoning the way we think we are. Mental processes we're not conscious of drive our decision making, while the kind of logical reasoning we believe our thinking should aspire to is really no more than a way to justify decisions we've already made. But it's not just our own thinking that is at issue. If we use logic to influence people unconsciously driven by emotion, we probably aren't going to be very successful in getting them to embrace our point of view.

While we've learned from mapping the anatomy of the brain that our minds operate differently than we thought, the mapping has also misled us into thinking that different mental functions reside in discrete areas of the brain. When we look at how information moves through the brain in real time, though, we realize that the way the brain works is a function of the relationships between the different areas, and that leads to some very strange happenings.

MIND OVER MATTER

At first glance, it's hard to make out what's taking place. On the screen is an image of the brain with different areas in different colors. The image is constantly changing, almost resembling a kaleidoscope, as the colors show us which areas of the brain are activated. As the functional magnetic resonance image (ƒMRI) records the heightened neural activity, what we are seeing is tangible evidence of those intangible thought processes that make up our minds, and what it tells us is stunning.

Before the invention of the ƒMRI, the inability to see the brain in action held back the progress of neuroscience. Although the electroencephalogram (EEG) became available early in the twentieth century, it measures only the gross electrical energy given off by the brain. But the ƒMRI enables us to get a much more detailed view. By tracking the flow of blood carrying glucose and oxygen to regions of the brain that are active, it effectively provides a moving picture of the brain at work. Seeing the flow of information through the brain has taught us that many of the functions formerly believed to reside in one area are actually a product of the interaction between different areas. From perception to thought, things are not quite as simple as we believed them to be.

Our sense data of the outside world is represented in the digital on/off firing of nerve cells in an area of the brain known as the sensory cortex. This pattern of firing is then compared to memories of similar patterns, allowing us to recognize what we have perceived. This is straightforward enough. But the ƒMRI shows us that as the sense data is registered, the areas of the brain responsible for emotions, goals, and high-level ideas are also activated. Only then do we find activity in the prefrontal cortex, the seat of consciousness. What we finally become aware of is a re-creation of the world shaped by everything else going on in the mind, from our feelings to our aspirations.

Our most dominant sense, vision, is the best example of how our experience of the world is processed by the brain. The commonsense view is that an image is projected on the retina by light bouncing off an object and entering the eye. The image then travels up the optic nerve into the brain and we "see." But the *f*MRI shows us that this is not what happens. An image projected on the retina doesn't travel as an intact whole, as if through a pipe, into the brain.

Rather than responding to the part of the image projected on it, the cells of the retina are quite specialized and fire only in response to specific aspects of the image, such as color and contrast. In addition, there is a blind spot right in the middle of the retina where the optic nerve is attached, and it has to be filled in. The image projected on each retina is broken down into 127 million discrete bits of information that travel up the optic nerve to the brain's primary visual cortex as a pattern of electrical signals.

Once there, they are processed by over a billion neurons in two dozen different areas. Some of these neurons respond just to orientation, others to direction, and still others to color. As the information moves out of the primary visual cortex, it is broken down into two further streams for processing, one for motion and one for the recognition of objects. Finally, these different aspects of vision are reassembled into a coherent perception.

Scientists call the areas where the reassembly takes place *convergence zones*, and they identify a hierarchy of them. At one level, all of the visual data converges. At another, higher level, the data from all of the senses comes together to form an image of the outside world. Our sight of a baseball game, the noise of the crowd, and the smell of peanuts and beer all converge to create our experience of the game.

But it's not just sense data that converge. In order for us to recognize an object, the information from our senses must be compared with previous experience encoded in our memories. Once that happens and the image is finally structured and recognized, we become conscious that we are seeing. However, what we see is not a mirror image of the outside world. It is made up of bits of information reassembled, in the view of one neuroscientist, "according to a person's memories, past experiences, and possibly even wishes."

Because we construct our reality but don't believe we do, our view of a situation will inevitably be subjective, and so will everyone else's. With all of us unwittingly operating off of our personal versions of reality, conflicts are inevitable. Employees and managers will see things differently, and so will customers and suppliers. We can't assume that our actions and words will be interpreted the way we mean them, nor can we assume that we're correctly interpreting the actions and words of others.

THE WIRING OF IDEAS

Fortunately, neuroscience also teaches us how to be more effective in the world we work and live in, regardless of its nature. Like every organ of the body, the brain is made up of cells, approximately 100 billion of them. Unlike the cells of other organs, though, neurons connect to one another and transmit signals in potentially 40 quadrillion different ways. To appreciate a number this large, consider that it would take more than 125 million years to count all of the connections. On average, each neuron is connected to one thousand other cells. It is these connections that are responsible for the brain's enormous complexity.

Neurons make up the wiring of the brain. Information travels from one end of the neuron to the other in the form of an electrical charge. The real action, though, is not in the individual cells, but in the connections between them. Most neurons are not linked directly together. Instead, there is a small, fluid-filled gap separating them called a synapse. When the electrical charge reaches the synapse at the end of the neuron, chemicals known as neurotransmitters are released and travel across the gap to the neuron receiving the signal.

Anything that affects the production and action of neurotransmitters alters the way the brain works. We've long known that this is the case with substances such as alcohol, caffeine, and antidepressants like Prozac, but now we're discovering that everything from exercise to mood has the potential to change how we think. If we're happy, our brains operate differently than if we are sad. Stress, pain, and sexual arousal will not only affect how input is processed, but how it will be associated with other perceptions and thoughts. We can affect the quality of our thinking in profound ways by consciously altering our mood or physical state, which in turn will also change the nature of our reality.

Because of the synapses and neurotransmitters, the wiring of the brain is constantly changing, and so are the mental processes it produces. Older synapses are dying off, new ones are being created, and existing ones are either strengthening or weakening. Neuroscientists are fond of describing the cause of synaptic death as a case of "use it or lose it," and the creation of new connections as "neurons that fire together, wire together." Altering synapses is how the brain rewires itself in response to what's going on in the environment, increasing the chances of a fit between the capabilities of our minds and the changing demands of the world we find ourselves in. Rewiring is how we learn.

On a practical level, the more a mental process is used, the stronger it becomes. The more I practice the violin, the more I reinforce the neural pathways required for violin playing. The more I use certain thought processes, the more habitual they become. The more I think a given idea, the more it shapes the environment of the mind. In his study of sea snail neurons, Nobel laureate Eric Kandel found that just one instance of firing changes the chemistry of the synapse and lowers the threshold for subsequent firing, but the effect quickly dissipates. After five instances of firing, though, structural changes occur that create a long-term memory. Even at a cellular level, practice makes perfect.

The chemistry of the synapse explains why repetition is important to master a skill or to ensure that facts are retained in memory, and it explains why we can become prisoners of habitual patterns of thinking. It also suggests that exposure to different kinds of stimuli can create new neural networks that broaden our thinking.

Because the world you know is essentially just a network of ideas created by electrical charges and chemical reactions, it can be affected by the electrical charges and chemical reactions of other networks. These networks are organized hierarchically in what Damasio describes as a "supersystem of systems." Higher-level networks with a large number of connections key the firing of those at lower levels.

The ideas represented in those high-level networks, such as values and deeply held beliefs, will drive both ideas and behavior at lower levels that are in harmony with them. If I believe in the idea of equality, I will see other people as equals and behave toward them accordingly. Recent data suggests that changes driven by high-level networks are longer lasting and more comprehensive than those that originate at a lower level. Using cognitive therapy to treat mental illness by changing how patients think has proven more effective than the use of either drugs to reset synapses or behavior modification techniques. In practical terms, if we get the big ideas right, everything else will follow.

This runs up against common practice in the business world, where the focus is on managing behavior. According to neuroscience, such an approach will be much less effective than using ideas to change the thinking that drives the behavior. If you want to improve customer service, you're better off stressing its importance and linking it to an employee's values than prescribing a set of behaviors that will probably be executed with indifference or contempt. Behavioral approaches are more suited to those animals that don't live in mental worlds of their own making.

SWAPPING PARADIGMS

We can think of our versions of reality as movies, and they don't just differ in small, nuanced ways. Although we believe we're viewing the same event, you may actually be watching the Disney version, while mine is by Alfred Hitchcock. The different movies drive different thoughts and actions. Yours may be humorous and prompt happy thoughts and laughter. Mine may be threatening and key my autonomic nervous system to ready my body for defense.

Our movies must always make sense to us. If anything occurs that doesn't fit the story line, our internal editor goes to work. Without our being aware of it, our editor determines what stays in the final version and what is cut or changed, resolving any conflicts between dissonant pieces of information.

Cognitive neuroscientist Michael Gazzaniga believes that the internal editor is our reason and is probably resident in the left hemisphere. He illustrates how the editorial process works when he describes a visit to a patient at Memorial Sloan-Kettering Hospital in New York City. This woman had suffered a lesion to the area of the brain responsible for spatial location, but testing had established that all of her other brain functions were normal. When he first met her, she was lying in bed reading the *New York Times*.

During the course of an interview in her hospital room, Gazzaniga asked the woman where she was. She replied that she was in her house in Freeport, Maine. When he asked how she could explain the bank of elevators outside her door, she answered, "Doctor, do you know how much those cost to have installed?" She wasn't joking. In her version of reality, she really was at home with her bank of elevators. To us, she's "making it up as she goes along." To neuroscientists, that's just the point. We all make it up as we go along.

Not all versions of reality are created equal. Some are a better fit with our experience than others, so they lead to more effective actions. If Gazzaniga's patient had attempted to leave the hospital and navigate through New York City as if it were Freeport, Maine, she would have been in for a series of very rude awakenings. What we've realized from tracing the path of information through the brain is that the paradigm, or theoretical framework, we've been using to understand how the mind works and how humans interact with one another isn't a very good fit. As a result, the actions we take based on that paradigm don't produce the results we intend; often they produce exactly the opposite.

The biggest hurdle to understanding and utilizing the discoveries of neuroscience is the self-perpetuating nature of paradigms. Although they are just our *versions* of reality, we mistake them for reality itself, and have a hard time believing that they're not the same as everyone else's. This makes it difficult for us to appreciate their effect, let alone entertain the notion that we could shift from one to another. While the idea that our minds create our reality has been with us for thousands of years, it is only within the last decade or so that neuroscience has made available the kind of hard data our logical minds accept as proof.

At some level, all of us know about paradigms or at the very least have experienced their effect. Our different political, social, and religious positions are the result of different paradigms. Conflicting paradigms are often the cause of our frustration with our spouses and children, or their frustration with us. At work, such conflicts are what makes it difficult for manufacturing to get what marketing is saying, and vice versa. While we may believe those we disagree with lack the breadth of vision and reasoning capability we have, it's more likely that they're just assembling the world in a different way.

But our experience of conflicting paradigms leads us to underestimate the significance of neuroscience's discoveries. It's not just on the level of our belief system, or our role in a family, or our professional orientation that paradigms operate. They structure our basic experience of reality: literally what we see and believe about the very nature of the world we inhabit. Because these kinds of paradigms operate at a very deep level, they drive not just different thoughts, but different ways of thinking.

The *objective* paradigm that is responsible for our common sense and logical thinking probably evolved from our early experience of the physical world. It works just fine when we're dealing with inanimate objects like rocks, stones, or clumps of dirt. But when we're dealing with animate beings, it doesn't work quite as well, and when it comes to people with minds like our own, it fails miserably. Our anticipation of how others will respond to our actions doesn't take into account our previous experience with them, their internal motivations, or their personal versions of reality—that is, if we even bother to think about their response at all when we act.

Twenty-first century managers know that their strategies must anticipate responses, that they must account for differing customer perceptions, and that their employees don't always see things the same way they do. But given the pace of business, they rarely have the luxury or opportunity to self-reflect. Our logical thinking is on automatic, and it's the default mode we use whenever we think about anything. Without being aware of it, we ignore interdependencies, past history, and conflicting points of view. It's simply the way our minds have evolved to work.

The adverse consequences of seeing people as inanimate objects and ignoring the way they interpret events aren't limited to human resource management. Every aspect of business, no matter how much our objective paradigm discounts it, involves thinking, self-determining people. Strategies are formulated by people, implemented by people, and responded to by people we call customers and competitors. Organizations are designed and staffed by people. Changing a business is about changing people. And lest we forget, companies are run by people we call managers.

Neuroscience offers us a paradigm for human interaction that recognizes humans as thinking beings capable of self-directed action. How they decide to behave is a function of the environment they find themselves in, their relationships with others, and their personal versions of reality. This *cognitive* paradigm gives us a better way of thinking about the complexity of human activity, by calling our attention to the dynamics of human relationships and the role of the mind.

It only makes sense for us to supplement our logic with a mode of thinking that accounts for what is so unique about human beings. When we do, our actions lead to much better results. Strategies that anticipate the challenges of being implemented by people and the responses of customers and competitors are going to reap a substantial competitive advantage. Organizations designed to implement strategies *and* to facilitate how people naturally work drive cost savings right to the bottom line. When management, in the words of Peter Drucker, stops "making it difficult for people to do their work," every hard measure of performance will rise dramatically.

Perhaps one of the most counterintuitive conclusions of the latest research is the way scientists believe the mind naturally makes sense out of the world. In spite of science's preference for fact over fiction, stories are seen not only as the way the mind works but as a better fit with human activity. Different points of view, relationships, and motivations are built into the structure of stories, so they do a better job of capturing the complexity of human interaction. Because stories as a way of thinking predate logic in the evolution of our culture and in the development of the mental abilities of children, we find them immediately accessible.

While logic and science have been responsible for the incredible improvement in the material quality of our lives, it has not been without a cost. The bias of our objective paradigm against stories is, as we shall see, responsible for the loss of valuable mental abilities, but neuroscience is helping us rediscover them. Besides, if objectivity is just an illusion, as neuroscience maintains, a story is as valid a way of making sense of our experience as a scientific theory. Both are just paradigms.

THE POWER OF IDEAS

Tracking the flow of information through the brain demonstrates that the world we inhabit is just a figment of the imagination. Playing a game of chance with four decks of cards shows that our emotions lead to better decisions than our reason. Understanding how a signal moves from one nerve cell to another teaches us that ideas can quite literally change the world. Our brief survey of the findings of neuroscience has demolished our reality, our reason, and our identity. But it has also taught us how really powerful ideas can be.

So much of what we've taken for granted turns out to be the opposite of what we thought it was. I don't produce thoughts; my thoughts produce me. The world isn't physical; it's mental. Objective logic isn't the best way to make decisions; incorporating our feelings is. It's not physical force that makes things happen; it's the power of ideas. The world neuroscience gives us is a very different place than we thought it was, and it demands different ways of thinking and acting.

Virtually everything we do now has to be seen through the lens of what we've learned about the mind. When it comes to how we approach business, we need to rethink everything we thought we knew about management. This isn't just about a new model for measuring a business, reengineering its operations, or motivating its people. This is about the nature of the world being different than we thought it was and about the need for a fundamentally different paradigm to drive the way we think and act.

From a world that exists only in our minds to a reasoning process that is only a justification for decisions we've already made, the world according to neuroscience does take some getting used to. But when we come right down to it, the fundamental lesson is quite simple. The power is in ideas. They can change the world and they can transform a business. All we need to do is open our minds and let them in. They'll do the rest.

FROM BRAIN TO MIND

The new owners of the ski area located on the edge of a small New England town wanted to build vacation condominiums, arguing that the resort would only be financially viable if they could ensure a large enough number of skiers would use it on a regular basis. This pristine village, virtually unchanged from colonial days, was now evenly split over the proposal and the discussions had grown heated. One side welcomed the jobs the proposed development would bring, but the other side resisted the idea of a housing development so out of keeping with the character of the town. Since the plan required a variance under the current zoning regulations, a town meeting was convened to vote on the request.

After the meeting was called to order, the developers were up first to present their case. Nicely bound handouts with the details of their proposal were stacked on the table in front of them, and attractive architectural drawings of the housing development were prominently displayed on easels on both sides of the stage. The condominiums were cleverly designed and landscaped to blend in with the surrounding woodlands. One couldn't help thinking that the developers had been in this situation before and had come to this meeting well prepared.

Everything about their presentation was professional and polished. Dressed in jackets and ties, they spoke persuasively and with compelling logic about how important the resort was to the economy of the town, and what would happen should it go bankrupt. They explained how many people currently used the resort, how many were needed to turn a profit, and how many the new condominium development would bring in. Detailed financial statements established both the necessity of the development for the economic health of the resort and the huge benefit it would bring to the town.

By the time the presentation was over, those opposed to the condominiums were feeling overwhelmed. They had nowhere near the resources of the developers to call upon, and it seemed as if every possible argument they had intended to make against the development had been preempted. Their major concern was that the character of the town would be irreversibly damaged by the increase in population and traffic, but it was difficult to marshal hard data to support the contention that the town would "feel" different and the quality of life would suffer.

When the moderator called for comments on the developers' presentation, the hall grew silent except for the sound of chairs scraping on the hardwood floor and a cough echoing through the room. No one was eager to stand up and speak for what looked like a lost cause. But then an old Yankee rose slowly to his feet. Dressed in a faded plaid shirt, worn corduroy pants, and a navy down vest, he moved so tentatively that he appeared incapable of mounting a credible challenge to what had just been presented. Sensing that if this was their only opposition, victory was inevitable, the resort owners settled more comfortably into their chairs.

Deliberately choosing each word, the old man started to speak. "I don't understand much about all these numbers," he said, "and you fellas do seem like nice people. But your argument for the condominiums reminds me of the man that just had to have a pickle to eat with his sandwich. He would take a bite of the sandwich and then a bite of that pickle. Another bite of the sandwich, and then another bite of the pickle followed. His lunch was the sandwich, and that should have been enough for him, but it wasn't. He always had to have that pickle to make what he called a 'complete' meal. Gentlemen, you're asking for one hell of a big pickle."

With that, he slowly sat back down again. The room was still and everyone seemed a bit puzzled by what had been said. Then a little bit of nervous laughter could be heard in the back of the room. Steadily it grew louder and louder and more widespread until finally becoming a roar that echoed through the room as people got the gist of what the old man had said. Although he hadn't countered any of the arguments the resort owners had put forth for the development, he had effectively changed the terms of the debate. The condominiums were no longer a financial necessity, they were one hell of a pickle that nobody really needed.

The comparison transformed how people saw the development. While there is nothing humorous about high-density housing, a pickle is kind of a silly food, and that probably occasioned a bit of the laughter. The word "pickle" also can denote a difficult situation, and that was picked up on as well. There was nothing logical about what the Yankee said—clearly the proposed condominiums didn't have anything in common with a kosher dill or a gherkin—so there was no rebuttal possible. The resort owners couldn't very well say the obvious, that the condominiums were not a pickle, because the old man had never asserted that they were. But from that moment on, the condominiums were referred to as "one hell of a big pickle."

They were never built, and the ski resort closed several years later. The owners, with all of their polish and formidable resources, had been defeated by a metaphor.

THE MIND ON METAPHOR

Being done in by a simple little rhetorical device like a metaphor would seem more fantastic if we didn't know from neuroscience how the mind works. After data from our senses is processed in the sensory cortex, it is compared to similar patterns of neural firing stored in memory, allowing us to recognize the new perception by its resemblance to others we have experienced before. The memory structures the perception, directing our attention to certain aspects of it and away from others.

A metaphor operates essentially the same way, comparing what we don't know to what we do. Perhaps the best known metaphor is Robert Burns's "My love is like a red, red rose." This metaphor asks us to understand the poet's "love," which we don't know, by thinking about it as something we do know, a "rose." The way we do this is to consider the attributes of the known rose and then look for correspondences in the unknown love. What immediately comes to mind is the stunning beauty and delicacy of the rose. By correlation, the poet's love can be understood as stunningly beautiful and delicate.

Metaphors also add a dimension that wasn't there before. Even though we can't personally know Burns's love, we are able to experience something similar because metaphors bring our senses into play. Because we don't just think the metaphor, but feel it, more mental processes are engaged than when we're just reasoning logically. Given Damasio's experiment on decision making, we can see why the "pickle" could have such persuasive power.

Both roses and pickles can change the way we see things, what we think about them, and how we act as a result. But there are also metaphors that operate on a much deeper level and have a more profound effect. Such metaphors determine the very nature of reality and how we think about it. Cognitive linguists George Lakoff and Mark Johnson contend that "our everyday reality," and "the way we think, what we experience, and what we do every day is very much a matter of metaphor." Even when we think we are using plain language and viewing our reality as it really is, these deeply embedded "conceptual metaphors" are structuring our perceptions and our thoughts.

According to historian of science Theodore Brown, the source of these conceptual metaphors that shape both our scientific thinking and our common sense is "our most ubiquitous physical experiences." Because we were animals living in a physical world before we developed consciousness, the physical we were familiar with became the source of the metaphors we used to make sense of our experience. This works fine as long as we're thinking about the physical world, but when we turn our thoughts to experiences that are not physical, our metaphors don't fit them. We distort our experience, use a mode of thinking that isn't appropriate, and then take actions that are ineffective.

While we can expect objects in the physical world to respond to our manipulation in straightforward and predictable ways, people with minds are capable of all kinds of machinations. They don't just react. They think about their experience and make decisions about how best to respond. They can lead us to believe they're doing one thing and do something completely different. They can strike an agreement with us one minute and go back on it the next. Or they can just leave us guessing about what they're going to do.

Since the world we inhabit is mental, according to neuroscience, ways of thinking and acting geared to the physical world are bound to fail, particularly when it comes to our interactions with other people. At the same time, other ways of thinking and acting that are effective in a mental world are never considered because we mistakenly believe we inhabit a physical world. As a result, much of what we do as managers is either suboptimal or self-defeating. We can become much more effective if we recognize this mismatch and ensure that our perceptions, thoughts, and actions fit the nature of the world we're operating in. The place to start is an understanding of the differences between the objective and cognitive paradigms and the worlds they create.

LIVING IN THE MATERIAL WORLD

The physical world was all early people knew, so of course it shaped their thinking. Whether they were reflecting on other people or their own mental processes, they saw them the same way they saw rocks, clumps of dirt, and trees. Interaction in this world of inanimate objects follows the model of one billiard ball colliding with another. The first billiard ball imparts force to the second, causing the second to move in a predictable way. With Newton's three laws of motion and relatively simple mathematics, I can even accurately predict where the ball will move. We needn't concern ourselves with the environment (beyond the surface of the billiard table,) or with the past relationship of the balls. After the initial impact, they no longer have an effect on one another.

This view of the world parallels the thinking of the Greek philosopher Aristotle. He believed that since the world was made up of separate objects, the right way to reason was to break things up into their component parts. By understanding the parts, we would then understand the whole. In Aristotle's world, "what you see and reason about is pretty much what you get." So we can also assume that we have no effect on what we are observing and our view is objective.

In the twentieth century, the objective billiard ball paradigm produced behavioral science, and it quickly came to dominate psychology. Because what you see is what you get, what goes on in the mind was not deemed suitable or necessary to be concerned with. When it came to motivating people, external force in the form of the stick or the carrot was all that was required. There was no need to consider intrinsic motivation, relationships, or the nature of the environment. Since it was such a simple model and advocated direct action, it appealed to pragmatic business managers. Behavioral science shaped, and continues to shape, management practice in the corporate world.

Of course, we've moved far beyond such a simple view. We know that people are more than just objects, that they have minds, and that their behavior is driven by their psychology. But metaphors are tricky things, and it's easy to fall victim to them. The physical world is our default source of metaphors and it continues to shape our perceptions of the world. If it didn't, the view neuroscience gives us wouldn't be so disconcerting.

IT'S ALL IN THE MIND

In the world we know, according to neuroscience, there are no things, only ideas. Physical objects interact according to Newton's laws of motion, but ideas without mass don't. Nor apparently do they obey Aristotle's laws of logic. In Damasio's experiment, the decision to choose from the lower-risk decks is made not as the result of syllogistic reasoning but because it feels like the best fit with the experience of past trials.

The biological anthropologist Robert Aunger sees this process of *fit* as the way the mind reasons about virtually everything. In contrast to Aristotelian logic, "our nonrandom, 'designed' solutions to problems are the result of a multistage mental tournament in which there is selection among blindly created variants for the strongest option, given the environment of thought at the time." Ideas vie with one another and the one that fits best with the situation under consideration, relative to the others, is the one we become conscious of.

We see this process of competition for *fit* everywhere in nature. Charles Darwin called it natural selection and believed it was how the natural world evolved. According to his theory, there are many more organisms in nature than there are resources to support them, so there is a competition among them to *fit* the demands of the environment. Those organisms that win the competition are *selected* to survive and pass their genes on to future generations.

Natural selection is not a static process. As a result of random mutations or recombination in sexual reproduction, genes evolve and produce organisms with different traits. If those traits enable the organisms to fit the demands of the environment better, their genes are passed on to subsequent generations. The environment also changes, selecting out different traits. Who we are today is simply the result of the chance mutations of our genes, selected because they enabled us to survive and procreate.

It's not surprising that the brain should operate the same way as natural selection, for even though mental activity may seem different, it is just a natural process. Our ideas are the products of the metabolic processes of living cells, and because these ideas create the mental world human beings inhabit, that mental world also operates through natural selection. In place of the inanimate objects that make up the physical world, we have animate beings with minds that move of their own volition.

This is what neuroscience's revolution is all about. The physical world is recognized to be mental, and the objective "billiard ball" paradigm is replaced by the cognitive "natural selection" paradigm. Rather than attend to objects and forces, we need to focus on relationships and the environment.

To think about this world, we're better served by the dialectical reasoning of Plato than the objective logic of Aristotle. While for Aristotle, it was the physical world that was ultimately real, for Plato it was the world of ideas. Because much of Plato's thinking anticipated the discoveries of neuroscience, he offers us a better way of reasoning for the world we inhabit, one that dovetails nicely with the way the mind actually works.

Plato was convinced that humans are inevitably subjective. When everybody has their own verson of reality, the best way to determine what's true is to play one person's point of view off of another's. The process of doing this is called a dialectic, and it is essentially a competition of ideas to arrive at a more comprehensive one that encompasses both. As we move from idea to idea, we rise up a hierarchy to the biggest idea of them all. Variously called "the good" or "the truth," it then informs all of our other reasoning and ensures that it is valid.

The dialectic fits perfectly with a brain that works through natural selection. There's Aungur's competition, a hierarchical organization, and a high-level idea at the top creating a mental environment that selects out other ideas in harmony with it. Instead of following an artificial method for reasoning that excludes what emotion and other unconscious processes can teach us, we just let the mind work naturally. When we need to solve a problem or make a decision, we specify the criteria for the outcome, freely generate options through brainstorming ideas that compete against one another, and then select the idea or ideas that fit our criteria.

Leaving aside the way we reason, comparing Aristotle and Plato as representatives of the physical and mental worlds gives us a sense of the kind of interaction with other people that works best in each. Both attempted to convince others of their ideas, and that's essentially what we do when we want other people to support us in the accomplishment of our goals. Aristotle made no effort to persuade because he assumed that reasonable men would be convinced by the superior force of his logic.

In contrast, Plato used questions to encourage people to reach their own conclusions, though he did subtly shape the mental environment that determined what those conclusions would be. While this is not the direct control that we think we have in the physical world, it is probably the most effective way of "moving" people.

Thinking and acting in line with the nature of the world we live in doesn't require learning a new set of algorithms to replace the logical ones we've grown up with. That's the beauty of the way the brain works. All we need to do is think about the cognitive paradigm and it becomes embedded in a neural network. Our minds will then randomly generate ideas and actions that fit with it. In fact, what we've done in the last few pages is create such a neural network. Now we just need to let our minds work the way they naturally do.

A PARADIGM IN TIME

Increasingly, a wide range of cognitive scientists building on the discoveries of neuroscience have concluded that the human mind really works through stories. As cognitive scientist Mark Turner puts it, "Story is a basic principle of mind. Most of our experience, our knowledge, and our thinking is organized as stories." Much like the importance of ideas and the hierarchical arrangement of the mind, this is a notion dating back to the ancient Greeks and only now, over two millennia later, being substantiated by science. Stories were the preferred mode of making sense of the world before Aristotle and others "invented" logic.

Even today, stories are so pervasive in our culture that their presence is not always recognized. We don't necessarily notice that our nightly news is in the form of stories or that there's inevitably a story behind a sporting event or one or more of its key players. We have story stocks, corporate stories, and the conflicting stories opposing lawyers spin around a given set of facts. We have the stories our kids tell about why their homework wasn't done, and we have the stories our elected officials tell us about why a given foreign or domestic policy is necessary. For a culture that values fact over fiction and sees logic as the right way to think, we tell a lot of stories.

Or according to the philosopher Daniel Dennett, it's the other way around. "Our tales are spun, but for the most part we don't spin them; they spin us." Rather than telling stories, it's as if we are handed a script and must act the role that it defines for us. Because of this, when we encounter a story, we almost immediately identify with the main character, internalize his or her worldview, and move toward taking it as our own. This gives stories much greater power to shape the way we think than a logical argument. They structure our experience, determine how we think, and drive the way we act. As "moving picture paradigms," they select what we attend to and what we ignore, so that our perceptions conform to the story and it becomes our reality.

Even beyond their impact, stories as a way of making sense out of the world have advantages over logic and are much better suited to the mental world we inhabit. Because they are another's perspective on the world, we are forced to acknowledge that others have different perceptions than we do, preventing us from falling into the trap of thinking that we're just objectively recording what's going on. Attention to the environment and relationships are also inherent in the structure of a story. The setting frames the action, which is driven by the conflict between the characters.

Just like metaphors, stories don't claim to be true, so they don't elicit attempts to logically refute them. They ask only that we entertain them as a way of organizing our experience of the world.

USING STORIES

Given the effect stories have on us, they are one of the most useful tools one can have in a mental world, replacing the carrot and stick of the physical world. We can use them both to understand and to shape how others think and behave. There's even evidence from neuroscience that empathy and storytelling are two sides of the same coin. Those afflicted with the physiological disorder known as dysnarrativia, an inability to tell stories, lose "the ability to read other minds, to tell what others might have been thinking, feeling, even seeing. Sufferers seem to have lost not only a sense of self but also a sense of other."

If we can tap into the story that someone else is telling, we can learn enough about them to anticipate how they'll behave. Just as when we perceive something by attending to a few clues and filling in the rest, so too are we able to infer from a minimum amount of information the stories others are telling. This is because, as H. Porter Abbott suggests, there are a limited number of "masterplots" that appear repeatedly in a given culture and help to define it. One prominent example is the Horatio Alger story, "a variation of the quest masterplot that speaks directly to cherished values in broad swathes of U.S. culture." In Horatio Alger's novels, by dint of hard work and good character, the young man overcomes obstacles and makes good. When we encounter elements of this plot, we're quick to fill in the rest of the story.

In addition to poor boy makes good, we have other masterplots, like bad man gets his just desserts, good man succumbs to tragic flaw, and boy meets girl and does or doesn't win her. But in the stories we're most likely to identify with, the hero is a good man or woman who does triumph in the end. It is the romance with the happy ending that sparks our interest, and the greater the achievement, the more power it has for us.

Just as with masterplots, we can identify different stock characters that appear repeatedly. "People of a particular character are expected to inhabit similar roles in different stories. We can develop a categorization of kinds of character—generous, selfish, brave, submissive, and so on." When we encounter some of the traits, we make an assumption about the character and their story and fill in the rest. Not too long ago, the *New York Times* ran a story suggesting that a new masterplot of our culture is "the rogue CEO." Martha Stewart and Ken Lay were named as the representative stock characters.

If we want to know how someone else is experiencing the world, we can try out different stories from our culture's stock and find the one that seems to fit the best with what we observe about their behavior, the way they speak, what they say, and anything else that might be available. If it's someone we're familiar with, we'll have even more information about them. We may know their family, their background, and even perhaps their hopes and dreams. We can then induce from this information a masterplot and character type. This will facilitate our empathy and understanding, and enable us to figure out how to motivate them to take the action we desire.

But it's not only others who can be viewed through stories. We, too, are defined by the masterplots of our culture. So we believe that if we work hard like one of Horatio Alger's heroes, we will be successful, and the masterplot guides our actions. While identifying the story that's defining us increases our self-awareness, we're not at the mercy of it. We can tell ourselves a different story that will change the way we think and behave.

Like any of our ideas or perceptions, stories are the mental products of neural networks with lowered thresholds for firing. The more we tell the story, the more the network is reinforced through structural changes in the synapses. If we stop telling a story, natural synaptic death will eventually weaken the network. If we tell ourselves a new story repeatedly, we'll create a new network with a lowered threshold for firing. It's really no different than learning a new skill through practice. The more the network is reinforced, the more the story becomes our reality.

The same is true for the stories of others as well. Although we've seen that we can't move ideas around in our minds as we do objects in the physical world, we can affect the environment of thought by telling a different story to embed a new neural network. Because of our shared masterplots and characters, the subtle use of just the right details is enough to change the stories people tell themselves. Mention the honest and hardworking man or woman, and people will fill in the rest of the Horatio Alger story.

Beyond their role in empathy, self-definition, and change, stories can also serve as examples or illustrations. Just like the metaphor of the man who wanted a pickle to go with his sandwich, we tell the story and let the audience draw their own conclusion, a conclusion we determine by the way we tell the story. Because of the natural tendency to identify with the character in the story, the moral will be felt as well as thought. Because everyone enjoys hearing good stories, there's a better chance that we'll have more of an opportunity to finish the story without interruption than we would with a logical argument.

But the use of stories shouldn't just be restricted to "people issues." Although logic encourages us to strip out feelings and focus on hard objective data, the kind of thinking the business world favors, Damasio's experiment made it clear such an approach is neither possible nor desirable. Business is not a purely objective pursuit—it is a human activity. When we analyze a business only in terms of what appears on an income statement or balance sheet, we're going to miss a lot. If we can figure out the story people are telling themselves, we'll know what's behind the numbers and be in a better position to take corrective action. The way to do that is to embed a new neural network by repeatedly asking yourself what story other people are telling.

A CAUTIONARY TALE

During the dotcom boom, I was asked by a client to assess a company they had acquired. Before the deal had closed, they had high expectations for this company. Although it operated in a small regional market, it had a solid staff and a loyal customer base. The thinking was that if the company sold and delivered the consulting services my client had pioneered, their growth would take off exponentially. Unfortunately, after the acquisition was completed, there was just one disappointment after another.

The consulting services my client had pioneered were so attractive that the company was growing by leaps and bounds. As the company got bigger, the board decided it was time to hire a new CEO to take them to the next level. She had a reputation as a financial wizard and was said to be able to accurately assess the potential of a company with just a quick look at the balance sheet and income statement. The board gave her a mandate to improve profitability and grow the business. She immediately set about "tightening the belt" and getting costs under control, and then she bumped up the marketing effort. Costs came down and demand increased. Rewarded by a healthy increase in the stock price for her efforts at improving profitability, she went shopping for acquisitions.

Within a quarter, she had her first candidate. Although the largely unknown regional player looked like a perfect fit, the CEO was a bit concerned about the "quirky" culture of the company. It was located in the southeastern part of the country and seemed to sponsor an unusually large number of parties for the slightest of reasons. She sensed a little belt tightening wouldn't hurt there as well. It was agreed that new managers would be brought in from the parent and the owners would leave as soon as the deal was done.

Expectations were high as the new managers were installed and the company shifted over to sell and deliver the new services. Even when the profit forecast for the next quarter was missed, there wasn't much concern. There were inevitably glitches when companies were merged. But the following quarter saw a dip in not just profit, but revenues as well. The CEO quickly took corrective action, sending a no-nonsense "fixer" down from headquarters to get things on track.

But revenues and profits weren't any better the following quarter, and it appeared that the downward trend was accelerating. Perhaps most worrisome was that the backlog of orders was shrinking dramatically. This defied all logic. Due diligence prior to the acquisition had established that there was a healthy customer base, and with the parent company's service offering, demand should have increased exponentially. Instead, it seemed as if the opposite was happening.

The CEO replaced the sales manager and sent down a team of the parent company's best marketers to address the falling demand. A large investment was made in a new ad campaign for the region and extensive training sessions for the salespeople. But it was all to no avail. At the end of the quarter, every significant indicator was on a downward trend. Worse yet, the marketers from the parent reported that the acquisition's sales and marketing teams were largely unresponsive. They would just sit in meetings and not say anything.

When it finally got to the point that the acquisition's results were hurting the parent company's performance and stock price, I was asked to pay a visit to the company. It was expected that I would study the company for a couple of weeks or so and then recommend whatever changes might be needed. Instead, after just one day, I found the cause of the performance problems. It was the parent company's hot new service offering.

The managers of the parent company were doing precisely what they had been trained to do. They looked at the key metrics of the business, and when they saw the downward trend, they instituted the logical corrective action. When overall results weren't what they should've been, a fixer was brought in who would not shy away from taking action, no matter how unpopular it might be. When the demand still wasn't there for the offering, they replaced the sales manager and increased the marketing effort. But without the backstory, my client never had a good handle on why the results were slipping. So they were not only just treating symptoms, they were doing it in a way that actually made matters worse.

I attended a sales and marketing meeting during my first day at the acquisition that was a case in point. A marketer from the parent company running the meeting spent the entire time in "Aristotelian mode," telling people what they needed to do. If anybody raised a concern, it was met with a recital of how wonderful the new service offering was and how successful the parent had become because of it. It wasn't long before no concerns were raised. When I asked one of the acquisition's salespeople if he'd ever been asked why results were down, his answer was no.

The staff from the acquisition prided themselves on working for a plucky little company. It was part of their culture to balance work and play, and as the saying in the company went, "there's always a reason to have a celebration." They had no interest in being stars, and the story they told themselves was about being good workers, good parents, and good citizens. They saw themselves as salt-of-the-earth people who worked hard but knew how to have a good time. The parent company was the conqueror from the cold and far too serious north. They put a stop to everything that had made working at the acquisition fun, and their confidence bordered on arrogance.

If the acquisition raised an issue about the appropriateness of what the parent company was telling them to do, it was quickly dismissed in a way that made people feel inferior. Soon, everyone started to resent the visitors from the parent company, and they weren't about to offer anything that might be helpful. Some joked that it was like the old television program about POWs, *Hogan's Heroes*. They might be conquered, but they were going to make it as difficult for the conquerors as they could. They were never asked, so they never offered to explain what was responsible for the company's problems. After a while, they just became passive.

The Aristotelian logic of the parent company obscured the real cause of the acquisition's poor performance. The hot new service offering was only hot in a given *environment* in *relationship* to a set of competitors. The parent company sold almost exclusively to Fortune 1000 companies, competing against large, established firms that weren't nimble enough to match the offering quickly. But the acquisition was in a region with no Fortune 1000 companies, and the smaller companies that were their market had no interest in the service. Besides, their regional competitors were quick to match any competitive offering. Since the acquisition had been instructed to sell the parent company's offering in place of their traditional services, they couldn't sell what people wanted and nobody wanted what they could sell.

After I presented what I had learned, the fixer and the marketers packed up and went home. The acquisition regrouped and went back to selling the services that had brought them success in the past. Eventually, the results improved, but there was never the big boost that had been anticipated when the deal was first done. After this hiccup, the parent company again continued to post enviable growth rates every quarter and to pursue acquisitions. Not much later, I was dispatched to Switzerland. Apparently, there were some cultural issues with the company's first international acquisition.

PARADIGMS AND THE POWER OF STORIES

Although we might see metaphors as just rhetorical ornamentation, they are fundamentally how the mind works. The sense data that are disassembled and reassembled in the brain are only meaningful when compared to something we are already familiar with. At the deepest level of the mind, conceptual metaphors act as paradigms and structure our experience of the world, determining what we see, how we think, and how we act. Perhaps because it was the experience we were familiar with before the development of our conscious minds, the inanimate physical world became the metaphor we use for how our minds work and people interact.

The common sense entailed by the objective paradigm distorts the world, leading to actions that are self-defeating, while obscuring others that would prove more effective. When we look at the way the mind actually works, we see that it operates just like Darwin's natural selection. Options are generated randomly and the mental environment selects out the fittest. Because the world we live in is mental, the cognitive paradigm is a better fit with how we think and act. Rather than use force to get people to do our bidding, we'll be better served creating a mental environment that will select out what we need them to do.

Stories are the way our minds naturally work, and they preceded the invention of logic as a way of making sense of the world. The stories we tell ourselves determine the way we view the world, the way we think, and the way we act. We can use stories both to understand people and to change their minds, and we can use stories as a framework to analyze a business, going beyond the numbers to the reasons for the numbers. In almost every situation we find ourselves in, stories give us a much deeper appreciation for the forces at work and how we need to address them.

THREE

WORKING RELATIONSHIPS

Two prisoners are accused of a crime and held in separate cells. The police don't have enough evidence to convict them, so they go to each prisoner separately and offer a deal. If the prisoner confesses and implicates the other, he will go free. If he doesn't confess, but the other prisoner does, he will get ten years in jail. If both prisoners confess, they will each get three years in jail. If neither prisoner confesses, they both will go free.

This is the setup for Prisoners' Dilemma, a favorite of game theorists and a staple of psychological research on relationships. It captures two essential truths about human beings. The first is that when we are involved in an interaction with another person, our behavior is interdependent. Actions we take will affect, and be affected by, the actions of the other. So any decision we make about what we do must take into account how the other person will likely respond, and vice versa. The second is that all of us are, first and foremost, looking out for our own interests.

From a logical point of view, each prisoner's decision about what

to do is a straightforward calculation of the relative costs and benefits. If the first prisoner confesses and the second doesn't, the first
prisoner will go free. If the first prisoner confesses and the second
does too, both will get three years. So the choice to confess yields
either three years or freedom.

If, on the other hand, the first prisoner doesn't confess and the
second doesn't as well, both will go free. But if the first prisoner
doesn't confess and the second does, the first prisoner will get ten
years. So the choice not to confess yields either ten years or freedom. Because neither prisoner knows what the other is going to do,
the safe, rational choice is to confess. An outcome of three years in
jail or freedom is a better deal than an outcome of ten years in jail
or freedom. But because a confession by one prisoner puts the other
prisoner at a disadvantage, their interests are in conflict.

This is not unlike many relationships we find ourselves in at work,
where cooperation with our peers will improve the performance of
our group and benefit us in the long term but where we are also in
competition for promotions and incentive compensation. While we
may keep the good of the enterprise in mind and desire a cooperative
relationship, we can't just blindly trust that our peers will be thinking
the same way. Nor can they trust that we will want to cooperate.

In Prisoners' Dilemma, with no way to communicate with one
another and with just one decision to be made, there is no logical way
for either prisoner to forge a cooperative relationship that benefits
both and beats the game. But in real life, there is almost always an
opportunity to communicate, and the relationship is rarely "one-off."
Usually, there are repeated interactions over time.

To mirror this more realistic situation, researchers have come
up with an iterated version of the game with multiple rounds. Each
prisoner's decisions for any given round can then take into account
the decisions made in previous rounds and those that will be made

in subsequent rounds. At the same time, the prisoners' decisions can be used to communicate how they intend to play the game. With multiple rounds and the ability to signal intent, it becomes possible to turn the competitive relationship into a cooperative one.

So how should the iterated version of the game be played? Because the rational choice is to confess, the challenge for either prisoner is to figure out how to change the other's decision from "confess" to "don't confess." Let's say the first prisoner confesses. If the second prisoner then confesses as well, both are locked in a competitive downward spiral. If, on the other hand, the second prisoner doesn't confess, it simply reinforces the first prisoner's decision to confess. This is the dilemma.

The solution is for either prisoner to start out not confessing, in order to send the message that the two should cooperate. Given the rational calculation, this is counterintuitive. If the other prisoner gets the message and doesn't confess in the next round, then the relationship has been changed into a cooperative one. If, however, the other prisoner still insists on confessing, then the prisoner who didn't confess now confesses to send the message that there will be consequences for the competitive behavior. This is also counterintuitive because the prisoner is competing to become cooperative. In the following round, though, he goes back to not confessing to signal the intent to cooperate.

Political scientist Robert Axelrod solicited computer programs from game theorists to play an iterated version of Prisoners' Dilemma. After running close to two hundred rounds, the program that did the best employed precisely this strategy. Called tit for tat, it aims for cooperation but matches competition with competition so you can't be taken advantage of. To always compete locks you into the disadvantageous downward spiral. To always cooperate just complements and reinforces the competitive behavior of others.

The game demonstrates that either party in a relationship has the ability to change it from competitive to cooperative. In the world created by the objective paradigm, the tit-for-tat strategy will strike us as illogical because we tend to see ourselves as separate individuals and our actions as unrelated to those that come before and those that follow. But in the world structured by the cognitive paradigm, our focus is on relationships between people over time, so such counterintuitive strategies come readily to mind.

But our story isn't over just yet. In a twist on the original setup, researchers divided people who were to play the game into two groups. One heard a news story about a clergyman who donated a kidney and the other heard a news story about a clergyman who committed a murder. When they then played the game, those that heard the story about the donation of the kidney were much more willing to cooperate. In the physical world, hearing such a story couldn't possibly change the logic of how to play the game. In the mental world, an idea can change everything.

RELATIONSHIP EFFECTS

In keeping with the goal of being objective and unemotional when it comes to reasoning, the corporate world tends to use its Aristotelian logic to separate the people from the business issues. The relative importance of each is signaled by the bias in the terms that are often used to contrast them. Plants and equipment are "hard" assets, while people are "soft" assets. Financial, strategic, and operational skills are "hard," but those used in dealing with people are "soft."

In most organizations, the soft, people issues are stripped out of the business and become the province of the Human Resources function, with its correspondingly lower status and compensation scale. This supposedly frees line managers to spend their time on the more important business issues. When I ran Training and Development for a large corporation early in my career, I was complimented by one line manager for being "not bad for a human resources guy."

Yet for the more than two decades that I have consulted on the formulation and implementation of strategy, people problems have been behind the majority of the issues I've been called upon to address. I was hired by a large Midwestern bank to help them reformulate their strategy and redesign their organization, but the impetus to bring in a consultant, I later found out, was a running battle between the CFO and CEO. My work developing the management skills of physicians at a leading HMO was driven by the CEO's struggle to manage his relationship with the president. The redesign of a generic pharmaceutical company's R & D process was necessitated by the manager's inability to relate to his diverse and highly educated staff.

The importance of the people issues and managers' discomfort with them was really brought home to me when the highly skilled head of a successful high-technology company retained me because he "wasn't very good at dealing with people." This man was a brilliant strategist, a talented operator, and genuinely beloved by all of his people. Yet he bought 25 percent of my time for three years to be on call just in case his relationship with any of his managers soured. He felt just fine handling every aspect of a very complex business, but when it came to people, he wanted a backup available.

No matter how we might deny it, relationship issues are the most difficult problems we face in business. Most neuroscientists now agree that our oversize brains evolved as an adaptation to help us function in a social environment. In fact, among primates there is a direct correlation between the relative size of the brain and the average size of their social groups. Contrasting how our two paradigms drive the way we think about the interaction of animate beings shows why.

In the physical world, I hit one billiard ball with my cue stick, and it hits a second ball, imparting force and, we assume, causing the second ball to move. According to systems theorist Ervin Laszlo, this Newtonian view is then carried over to the world of living beings "so that when we speak of the 'response' of a living thing to an 'external stimulus,' we seem to be talking about something like what happens to a billiard ball when it is hit by another." But, of course, this isn't the way relationships work between thinking, animate beings.

Let's say I'm walking down a path in the woods when I encounter a snarling dog blocking my way. With my best logic, I determine that a swift kick with sufficient force will move the dog a reasonable distance out of my way. But this reasoning doesn't account for how my relationship with the dog at the present moment is affected by our previous interactions and the way both of us think. It isn't just the Newtonian force of my kick that causes the dog to move, it's how the dog's mind interprets my kick and uses its own energy to respond. The immediate goal of my kick may have been to get the growling dog out of my way, but its effect goes beyond my immediate goal.

When it's kicked, the dog might be frightened and run away, or it might be angered enough to turn and attack. If it bares its teeth at me as a warning to quickly vacate the area, I will then respond, depending on how I interpret the bared teeth and my own tolerance for pain. Perhaps I'll charge the dog and then stop, attempting to frighten it away. Maybe the dog will run away at that point, or maybe it will conclude that it wants to engage in battle and attack. In either case, I have decisions to make based on the dog's behavior, and it has decisions to make based on mine.

It makes no sense to view the parties to this interaction as independent, for the actions of one are based on the actions of the other. After the first billiard ball hits the second, we can pretty well conclude that they are done with each other. But my relationship with the dog is a circuit of repeated interactions, with each one affected by the previous ones and affecting those still to come. These interactions can lead to a competitive escalation of the battle until both man and dog are bloodied. Or they can fall into a complementary pattern where my aggressiveness and the dog's deference (or vice versa) reinforce each other.

This view of the interaction adds critical insights obscured by logic. We recognize that how each of us act is a function of the relationship, so before we decide on a course of action, we need to anticipate what the response of the other will be and then decide what we will do. We also see that what happens at a given moment in time is not an isolated event, but is a product of the past and will have effects in the future. We appreciate that the current state of a relationship is the result of the interaction of its parties, and that a change on the part of one will be compensated for by a change on the part of the other.

Relationship effects are quite understandable when seen through the lens of the cognitive paradigm, but they often surprise the logical mind as unintended consequences. Applying sufficient force to the dog with a good, solid kick should send it on its way, but it's a relationship effect when it comes back snarling in response. Appreciating such effects enables us to anticipate how animate beings will respond to our actions and to gain an advantage by leveraging them.

When the interaction is between people, it gets even more complex. Now we have to take into account those high-level ideas that drive decisions on how to act. Maybe the person I'm interacting with has just heard a news story about a clergyman donating a kidney, or maybe they've just been dressed down by their boss and are looking for a target for their aggression. Either way, logic isn't going to help me figure out what to do, but the kind of thinking entailed by the cognitive paradigm will.

Early in my career, I was invited to give a presentation of my company's capabilities to a division of Citigroup. This was an opportunity to sign up an extremely desirable client. It was *the* bank at the time, with a reputation for being far more aggressive and cutting-edge than other banks. There was also a touch of arrogance that went along with their success, and they were known for being tough people to do business with. But my work with them would not only be lucrative, it would be a great reference to use with other prospects. I must admit that I was both nervous and a little awed when I entered the division's posh offices on Park Avenue.

As I was waiting in a reception area while the staff attended to other business, I spent the time going over my presentation. I wanted it to be as crisp and polished as possible. I had worked hard to make sure the materials were the best they could be, and I'd invested a lot of time practicing it to ensure that I would come across just the way I wanted to. Finally, after what seemed an eternity, I was invited into their conference room.

Even before I had a chance to sit down, one of the executives expressed his conviction that I couldn't possibly be of any use to their division. He asked what kind of experience I could have that would be of value to a business as complex as theirs. But I never had a chance to answer that question, or any others for that matter. It didn't seem to make much of a difference because the questions were just rhetorical, and nobody seemed interested in what I had to say about anything. They were much more interested in what they had to say, and most of it had to do with how inexperienced and incompetent I was.

Every time I tried to get a word in, I was interrupted. The copies of my carefully produced presentation sat in front of me, never used. The abuse just went on and on, until finally there was a pause when they appeared to have run out of steam. It was now my turn, but given the relationship effects, I knew that I'd get nowhere arguing against them. Thinking back to Prisoners' Dilemma, I wondered if it wouldn't be better to do the opposite of what they expected and agree with them.

So I began with, "Gentlemen, if you'll give me a minute, I'll explain why you're right and I'm absolutely not the person to do this work for you." As soon as the words were out of my mouth, they were on me again. Only this time, they were arguing that I was the one they needed to do the work for them, and they were no less insistent than they had been before.

Perhaps they were enjoying a game of Pick on the Consultant, or maybe they just wanted someone to take their frustration out on. Whatever the cause, they were ready to counter anything I was going to come up with. Because I acted counterintuitively and cooperated rather than competed, I leveraged the relationship effect, and they ended up making my argument for me. It didn't hurt that their self-images demanded that everyone had to be seen as eager to work with them. It marked the beginning of a long and lucrative relationship.

THE THEORY OF MIND

Doing business seems much more complicated in the world according to brain science. In the world of logic and common sense, I can just do what I want with no more concern for relationships and mind-sets than a billiard ball has. But now science teaches me that my actions are constrained by the relationships I find myself in and that I have to account for how others think. Thankfully, though, my brain is naturally configured to work just the way neuroscience tells me it must.

There are a special kind of nerve cells in the brain called mirror neurons. They are one of the most recent discoveries of neuroscience, and they're generating a lot of excitement because they explain everything from our acquisition of language to how we learn new skills. They were first discovered in macaque monkeys when it was observed that the same premotor neurons fired whether a monkey performed an action or just observed others doing it. Mirror neurons have since been discovered in human beings, but there are subtle differences in our version of them.

In monkeys, the action must be goal-directed, but in human beings that's not necessary for the mirror neurons to fire. In humans, the prefrontal cortex is also involved, and it enables us to copy more complex actions and capture intention. Activity in our brains not only mirrors someone moving across the room, it mirrors how the person moves—dancing steps of the tango for instance—and it mirrors the intent—to teach the steps. We not only mimic the action in our minds, we mimic the mental state that leads to the action. It appears that there are mirror neurons for emotions as well. Because they are absent in children with autism, researchers believe that they are key to the development of social skills.

The discovery of mirror neurons provides a biological basis for what is known as the theory of mind. First identified in the late seventies, this is our ability to appreciate that other people have minds, just as we do. We are not only able to recognize that their intentions, desires, and goals may be quite different from ours, but to accurately predict what they are. The theory of mind appears to develop in children by age four, and it, too, is missing in people with autism. However, it is not flawless. We tend to apply it to our pets, other animals, and even to geometric shapes that appear to move intentionally.

We call what mirror neurons and the theory of mind enable us to do empathy. More than any other species, we have evolved the ability to step into others' shoes and see and feel the world from their perspective. It's easy to see how this would grease the skids of social interaction and enable us to more effectively negotiate the world we live in. It's also easy to see how, if we make use of this talent, we can be more successful in managing our business relationships.

We don't have to struggle to try to understand the perspective of others, because our brains automatically mimic the firing patterns of their brains. We don't have to worry about what story they're telling, because our brains are automatically producing the same story. We don't have to guess what action we need to take to get the response we desire, because our response will be theirs. All we have to do is just let the mind work naturally. However, there are a couple of hitches in the system.

It's been said that before you can step into another's shoes, you have to take your own off first. We have a tendency to get stuck in our own perspective and project it on other people. This inability to suppress our own perspective leads to errors in understanding others, and the errors seem to be greater the more different other people are from us. While there are lots of reasons for our failure to suppress our view, there is an easy fix.

Experiments have shown that we are capable of using our conscious minds to reappraise an emotion and change the way we feel. When subjects were shown a picture of a woman crying, they initially experienced negative emotions, but when they were told that she was crying tears of joy after her wedding, brain scans showed decreased activity in those regions of the brain responsible for emotion. This is the result of the prefrontal cortex releasing the neurotransmitter serotonin that dampens the activity of the amygdala.

This same kind of reassessment can enable us to suppress our perspective. If we believe that it's important, we can consciously shift our attention to focus on the perspective of another person. However, because ideas change the processing in our minds, learning about mirror neurons and the theory of mind will itself dispose our minds to unconsciously suppress our own perspective for that of another.

Reappraising a situation also requires seeing it as something other than it currently is, and it is our imaginations that enable us to do that. In the Aristotelian universe, what you see is what you get, and imagination is neither prized nor cultivated. But in the mental world, things become what we imagine them to be, and imagination is given free rein. When we accept the validity of the cognitive paradigm, it becomes easier to consciously shift our attention and make use of our imaginations.

THE CONSTELLATION OF RELATIONSHIPS

Although our brain has evolved so that we're well equipped to empathize, in order to benefit fully from our mirror neurons and innate theory of mind, we have to believe that it's important to manage our relationships. In the conventional view, there is one managerial relationship, and it is with employees. But if managers are going to be successful, they also need to proactively manage their relationships with customers, suppliers, peers, and their bosses. Asking questions can help us learn more about other people's views, and stories can help us to manage our relationship with them.

While a well-designed product or service, efficient operations, and skilled management are all nice to have, they are of no value without paying customers. But if you have customers, you can get everything else you need. Although it's just reasonable that you should do everything you can to satisfy them, there's a built-in conflict between customers and suppliers. Customers want as much as they can get for as little money as possible, while suppliers want to give as little as possible for as much money as they can get. Add the fact that customers often seem to be an intrusion into an organization and an interruption of the important work we do, and reasonable behavior goes out the window.

So we need to consciously put aside our perspective, adopt theirs, and then treat them the way we want to be treated as customers. It may seem simplistic, but the key to satisfying customers is to ask them what they want and then give it to them. At the same time, we need to guard against doing things that might increase our profit in the short term, but cost a customer in the long term. L.L. Bean is legendary for accepting any item for return, including a set of snow tires that weren't even bought at the store, and desk clerks at the Ritz-Carlton have the authority to significantly reduce bills for dissatisfied customers. But my cell phone carrier locked me into a contract I didn't need and then didn't stand behind the phone they sold me when it failed. Who don't I do business with anymore?

Just as Damasio's subjects used emotion rather than reason to make their decision on what decks of cards to choose from, so too do emotions drive our purchasing decisions. We don't necessarily buy a car because it's the most cost-effective and reliable transportation. We buy it because it satisfies our desire for status, because we like its styling, or because we enjoy the thrill of going fast. The same way ideas can lead to an emotional reappraisal, they can change our view of a product or service, and they are most powerful in the form of a narrative. Once we've empathized with our customer, we can fit our product or service into their narrative or create a new, more attractive one.

When we're dealing with customers, all of us have the ability to go beyond what is required or to deliver less than the customer needs. It might be advice, technical support, timeliness, or payment terms that are within our discretion, and we exercise it based at least somewhat on how we feel about the customer. Our suppliers are in the same position. Rather than take them for granted or repeatedly try to beat them down in price, it makes sense for us to build a relationship in which they use their discretion for our benefit.

Since I'm in the business of delivering a professional service, I have a lot of discretion over what my customers receive. I always strive to do the best I can, but I do have decisions to make. When it's two in the morning and I'm exhausted, do I put in that extra hour of work, or do I call it a night? Do I make that seven-hour plane trip for a two-hour meeting my client wants me at, or do I conveniently have a scheduling conflict? Does my client get me so turned on about their business that neurotransmitters are released that speed up my mental processing and enable me to do better work?

The most successful CEOs I've ever worked with have gone out of their way to build a satisfying relationship with me. I'm usually offered something to drink when I meet with them in their offices, and more often than not, they are the ones who go and get it. They ask me about how my business is going and seem generally concerned. While they are careful to manage the budget for my work, not one has ever tried to force me to reduce my price. Perhaps most important, they convey a narrative about what they're trying to do with their business that gets me as excited as they are.

In any customer-supplier relationship, there is always the potential for the kind of dynamics we saw in Prisoners' Dilemma, and one of my clients did a brilliant job of managing them. About two months after I called on him, he phoned me up and told me that he'd decided to give my firm all of the company's consulting work. I was pleasantly surprised, but I asked him how he could know that we'd do a good job since he hadn't checked any references. He answered that he was sure we would, and if any problems occurred, the two of us would work together to solve them. I then protested that he didn't even know how much we charged. His response was that he was certain I would be fair. Maybe my mirror neurons started firing, but I couldn't help but return his trust in kind. I worked to do the best job I could for him, and I charged him the lowest fee possible. We worked together for almost fifteen years.

When it comes to peers, things get a bit dicier. Sometimes they're our customers, while at other times they're our suppliers. Even when they're neither, a comment dropped to the boss can hurt us or help us, and in the future they may become our boss or our employee. Still, the approach is the same as in any relationship. We want to empathize and use questions to ensure the perspective we assume is accurate. We want to understand their story and convey our own in a way that enlists their support. But we can't ignore the potential for Prisoners' Dilemma dynamics.

One of my peers on a project team once kindly volunteered to put the finishing touches on a report of our findings and recommendations. But when he gave the presentation at a meeting with our sponsor, he ignored what the team had come up with and presented his view as if it were ours. When our sponsor raised some of the same concerns I had raised, the peer replied that he too had the same concerns but had been overruled by the team! Naively, I had trusted him not to confess.

Axelrod's research concluded that we should start out trusting, and it does set a cooperative tone that hopefully the mirror neurons will mimic. But we can't be so trusting that we're taken advantage of. I'm sure my peer was telling himself a story that provided a moral justification for his dishonesty. My mistake was not to have built in any insurance. I still start out trusting, but I've learned to always be on guard against the inevitable pull of our selfishness.

Perhaps the most counterintuitive relationship to think about managing is the one with the boss, because the conventional wisdom holds that managing the relationship is their job. In the early 1980s, John Gabarro and John Kotter wrote an article for the *Harvard Business Review* entitled "Managing Your Boss." In it, they recommended asking the boss a series of questions about their needs, goals, and preferred working style, so that the boss could be managed like a customer. It was simple and brilliant. Ask what bosses want and then give it to them. While many employees feared that the approach might seem a bit presumptuous, handing an article to the boss with the imprimatur of the *Harvard Business Review* on it beforehand made it acceptable. Besides, all managers would love an employee who wants to make them successful.

Proactively managing relationships just makes it easier to get the job done, and the tools we need to do it are hardwired into the brain. As in so much of management according to the discoveries of neuroscience, all it requires is that we consciously direct our attention. Yet we do live in a world where Machiavelli is still read and venerated by some. On occasion, it's helpful to have some less intuitive tools at hand.

THE ART OF PERSUASION

From Plato's *Dialogues* to Dale Carnegie's *How to Win Friends and Influence People,* we have a long history of people offering advice on how best to get our way. Often people object that such tactics are manipulative and believe that there is something immoral about their use. But we've got to remember that the brain making these moral judgments evolved to enable us to get others to do what we want them to. Since the brain is wired to help us in that endeavor, the judgment of what is moral or immoral should probably be restricted to the ends and not the means.

The psychologist Robert Cialdini took a scientific approach to the subject in his book *Influence: Science and Practice,* and he has come up with six different tactics. Whether or not we can bring ourselves to use them on others, it's important to be aware of them because others will undoubtedly use them on us. Some of them are so fundamental to how humans interact, odds are we've used them without even being aware of it.

This is certainly the case when it comes to *reciprocation,* because it's the glue that holds social groups together. When people do something for us, we feel obligated to do something for them in return. When we're the first to do the favor, we accrue social capital that we can then call on later. Cialdini uses the example of one subject in an experiment giving a soft drink to another and then later asking the person to buy raffle tickets. On average those that had received the gift of the soft drink first bought twice as many raffle tickets. If we do favors for people without being asked, we predispose them to respond to our requests for help later on.

We've seen that we strive to keep our version of reality consistent and will either suppress or rationalize any information not in keeping with it. We can use this psychological dynamic to our advantage by getting people to first agree to a position and then asking them to take an action that is in line with that position. Cialdini calls it *commitment and consistency.* There's an old sales technique that poses a series of questions that will certainly be answered in the affirmative and then follows up with a request to buy a given product. It goes something like this: "You love your family, don't you? You wouldn't ever want them to be unprotected, would you? If something happened to you, wouldn't you want them to be taken care of? You'll want to buy this life insurance policy, won't you?"

The reason this technique works is because of the hierarchical organization of ideas in the brain. As we've seen, those high-level ideas evoke thoughts and actions in harmony with them. To make use of this technique, we don't have to be as smarmy as the life insurance salesman. We can just establish agreement on a set of principles that will lead naturally to the action we desire someone else to take.

Because the brain is first and foremost social and because membership in our prehistoric groups was beneficial to our survival, we can use *social proof* to motivate desired behavior. We can think of it as peer pressure because it plays off our need to be accepted by others. The knowledge that those we want approval or acceptance from are doing something is a strong reason for us to do it as well. We can make use of this need by calling attention to how many people are engaged in a given behavior, or we can systematically build peer pressure by convincing people one by one until we've created a grass roots movement. Targeting high-status people, or thought leaders, first will work best.

Liking is perhaps the most intuitively obvious tactic, but also the one that seems most ignored in practice. When we like certain people, we are more willing to do what they want us to do. Because of this, it's worthwhile for us to spend the time to build friendly relationships before we need to call on someone for a favor. While the easy way to figure out how to build such friendships is just to consider what we like in a friend, there are some general principles. We like people who are like ourselves, so it's important to establish a commonality of interests. And we like people we spend time with. Then there's the one you learned as a child: if you want a friend, be a friend. We like people who like us, so we just need to like people, and they'll like us in return.

In more than two decades of giving management seminars, I have used the phrase, "the research shows," thousands of times, yet nobody has ever asked me what research. We have an incredible respect for *authority*. In a classic experiment, Stanley Milgram showed that when instructed by a researcher in a white lab coat, subjects were willing to administer life-threatening shocks to total strangers who gave the wrong answer to a question, even when they claimed to have a potentially fatal heart condition. But we have more respect for the authority that comes with expertise than the authority that comes with a position in a corporate hierarchy.

Cialdini's last technique, *scarcity*, might have its roots in the Darwinian struggle for survival in an environment of limited resources. Something about hearing that it's the last one available or that the offer is good for one day only drives us to action. This is the tactic that I have the most difficulty with. I see its use as primarily limited to customer relationships, and decisions made under its influence produce more than their share of buyer's remorse. As a favorite of car salesmen, it has a well-earned bad reputation.

Although these tactics do test as being effective, perhaps their use should be restricted to those times when we're trapped in a Prisoners' Dilemma dynamic or when we encounter disciples of Machiavelli. If we're really out to do the right thing not just for ourselves but for others, then we need only to embed a neural network of principle at a high level, and the right behavior will follow. We just make life more difficult for ourselves if we don't make use of our brain's innate ability to proactively build good working relationships before we have to call upon them.

PEOPLE

Deny it as we might, business is all about managing relationships. The objective paradigm leads us to believe that we can just pursue our goals without giving much thought to anything else. The cognitive paradigm, though, highlights counterintuitive relationship effects that can become self-defeating. In most of our relationships, there's another prisoner whose interests are both aligned with ours and yet in conflict.

The only thing for us to do is empathize with those we interact with, anticipate how they will act, and then select an approach that creates the response we want. At the same time, we have to keep in mind the other key relationship between the past, present, and future. Fortunately, our brains come equipped with the wiring to do so. Our mirror neurons, and the theory of mind they enable, allow us to quickly and effectively adopt the perspective of another.

First, though, we must suppress our own perspective, and that can require actively shifting our attention from ourselves to others. But again, the brain is wired to facilitate this. All we have to do is hold the thoughts in our minds that relationships are important and that we need to be proactive about managing them. Neuroscience's explanation of how our minds work is just the kind of hard data that convinces our logical minds to attend to relationships and put aside our own view in favor of that of others.

Rather than see ourselves living and working in a Newtonian world of billiard balls, we need to recognize the constellation of relationships that determine our success or failure in business. Our relationships with customers, suppliers, peers, and even our bosses should be managed proactively. To assist us in empathizing, we can make use of questions to gather information and garner commitment. Our innate ability to appreciate and tell stories gives us a deeper understanding of what motivates people and a means to predispose their minds to take the action we desire.

Our brains have evolved to facilitate social interaction, and we can trust them to give us the information we need to build good working relationships, but at times we may wish to avail ourselves of Cialdini's influence techniques. If nothing else, we need to be aware of them in a world where Machiavelli's *The Prince* is still selling robustly four centuries after it was written. But because they merely leverage the way the mind naturally works, we probably make use of most of them without even knowing it.

There is, of course, one relationship we haven't talked about—the one between the manager and the employees. While all relationships can be difficult because of the tension between cooperation and competition, the managerial relationship is complicated by power, which skews everything. What we might expect to work doesn't, while what does work is often counterintuitive. Once again, though, we're aided by the insights of brain science.

FOUR

MANAGING UPSIDE DOWN

"I watched, amazed, as she opened the refrigerator and various cupboards, found bottles and a glass, then poured herself a gin and tonic. She took the drink to the TV, turned the set on, flipped from one channel to another, then, as though in disgust, turned it off again. She selected a glossy magazine from the table and, still carrying her drink, settled in a comfortable chair. Occasionally, as she leafed through the magazine she identified something she saw, using the signs of ASL, the American sign language used by the deaf."

Why is enjoying a drink while viewing television or leafing through a magazine so amazing? Because Jane Goodall isn't watching a human being, but a chimpanzee named Lucy. Even after spending a lifetime studying chimps in the wild, the primatologist is still taken with how much they resemble us. When we see animals behaving like humans, it throws even our simplest acts into relief. It's like a metaphor, causing us to see in a new light what we've taken for granted. Because chimps are closely related to us and share over

98 percent of our genes, it's as if we're watching an earlier version of ourselves. It's particularly illuminating when it comes to relationships involving power.

Just like early human tribes of hunter-gatherers, chimpanzees live in bands of twenty to forty with a clear hierarchy and an alpha male at the top enjoying privileged access to food and mates. He becomes the alpha by being the strongest and maintains his position by cleverly creating the appearance of even greater strength through behavioral displays that cause him to look more ferocious than he is. He jumps up and down, shakes branches, and hurls rocks into the bush. The display throws the community into a chaos of pants and screaming.

The better his display, the greater the chance the alpha's intimidation will be successful and he won't have to resort to the risk of actual fighting to maintain his status. One alpha male, Mike, learned to kick four-gallon tin cans in front of him to make such a racket that no one would challenge him. Figan, an adolescent who would rise to alpha status himself one day, was seen practicing kicking cans in imitation of Mike.

No chimp in the band is untouched by the alpha's display of who's in charge, and each must determine how best to manage the relationship with him. Most of the lower-ranking males pay court. They approach cautiously, and when given the signal that it's safe, they kiss his thigh or lips, and then both engage in mutual grooming. Some may decide to challenge the alpha, in either overt or subtle ways. Just before his bid for alpha status, Mike nonchalantly turned his back on the reigning alpha during a display. Others just stay far away. But all "need highly developed social skills—particularly those males who are ambitious to attain high positions in the dominance hierarchy. Low-ranking chimpanzees must learn deception—to conceal their intentions or to do things in secret—if they are to get their way in the presence of their superiors."

It has become fashionable today to use the term alpha to describe the man or woman at the top of an organization, and it is questionable how far to take the parallel between humans and chimpanzees. Michael Gazzaniga notes that most male chimpanzee behavior is aimed at the goal of becoming the alpha male, and he believes that the same is true of humans. Anyone who has ever worked in a large organization has experienced the human version of displays, deception, withdrawal, and thigh kissing. The relationship with the alpha determines the quality of chimps' lives, and so they mobilize all of their social intelligence to compete, cooperate, or avoid. The same is true of humans and their managers.

The role of the manager in a large organization is fraught with problems, and when we see it as just a slightly more civilized version of alpha status, we can understand why. Whether we're a chimpanzee or a corporate employee, we don't like being controlled by others. Not many of us care for the boss, either, and most of the stories our culture tells about bosses are far from complimentary. There's Dagwood Bumstead's Mr. Dithers, there's Dilbert's pointy-haired boss, and there's Michael, the branch manager of Dunder Mifflin in *The Office*.

Even beyond the discomfort of submitting to the alpha, our standard management practices don't create warm feelings. The approach they entail is more suited to forms of life lacking the ability to think. Since they offend employees and become self-defeating, the most effective managers, according to neuroscience, are the ones who do the least in the traditional sense of management. But because those who are promoted to management are usually the high achievers in an organization, it's particularly difficult for them to back off. The solution is to turn the relationship upside down and redefine what it means to be the boss.

EXTENDING THE METAPHOR TOO FAR

Peter Drucker ranked Frederick Winslow Taylor's effect on the modern world with that of Sigmund Freud and Charles Darwin, yet Taylor is hardly a household name. Nor are the time and motion studies he pioneered quite on the order of psychoanalysis or the theory of evolution. It is Taylor, though, who is responsible for the way we manage.

Although he was the product of a wealthy Quaker family, Taylor chose a career as a machinist. He joined Bethlehem Steel, where he demonstrated a talent for improving the productivity of machinery used in making steel. His first major success came when he pioneered a process to produce superheated steel cutting tools that quadrupled the speed of lathes. But it was the common shovel that led to his fame and the transformation of management.

He was given the job of designing a more efficient shovel for men to load coal into blast furnaces, and he approached it like a scientist. He observed the men shoveling coal, measured how many pounds were in each shovelful, and calculated the total amount shoveled over the course of the day. He then experimented with different amounts of coal per shovelful, and found that twenty-one and a half pounds was just the right amount to keep the men working efficiently all day and moving the most coal. When he redesigned the shovel to hold that amount, the company was able to reduce the number of men shoveling coal from 500 to 140.

But Taylor realized that the design of the shovel was only one part of the productivity equation. The other part was how the men used the shovel. Applying the same approach he had used to improve the efficiency of machines to the people working on the machines, he broke the task down into its component parts, made careful measurements, and concluded that there was "one right way" to do the job. Those employing a fluid motion and putting both shoulders behind their thrust were clearly more efficient, so he taught all of the men to shovel that way, and there was another significant increase in productivity.

Managers had long been accustomed to reengineering their machines, but the human side of production had remained stubbornly resistant to any improvement attempts. This all changed when Taylor looked at the men as if they were machines. He called his approach Scientific Management, and managers found the application of scientific method to human work enormously attractive. Taylor quickly acquired an international reputation, and soon legions of his disciples could be found roaming through factories around the world with clipboards and stopwatches.

Taylor's approach wasn't limited to just industrial work. Every task in life could be performed more efficiently, he believed, even the domestic ones. The layout of the modern kitchen is the result of Scientific Management, and according to his wife, he also designed a better method for cooking eggs and baking pies. He is responsible for the idea that we should attend to the most efficient way of using our time and doing our work. From daily planners to our fear that we might be wasting our time, Taylor's influence is still felt far and wide.

He wasn't interested just in making more money for the owners of Bethlehem Steel. He envisioned himself as the savior of the workingman, and hoped that his Scientific Management would usher in a new age of cooperation between managers and employees. Rather than leaving them to fight over how big a slice each got, his idea was to increase the size of the pie. Just like Aristotle, he believed that men were reasonable beings and motivated by economic self-interest. It was only logical that if they were paid for the amount they produced in a given time period, they would eagerly embrace a more efficient way of working to improve their earnings.

However, those he was intent on saving didn't share this view. They had always had the freedom to do their jobs as they saw fit, and they took pride in their skill and independence. With Taylor's method, though, young men with college educations and stopwatches determined how the men would do their work. All that was important was that they precisely follow the process laid out for them. In the words of Samuel Gompers of the American Federation of Labor, Taylor reduced the working man to no more than a "cog in a machine."

Taylor's work redefined the role of the manager. He (it was nearly always he) became the brains of the organization, the one who determined how everything was to be done. But the more the manager did, the less the workers needed to do. Because he separated thinking from doing and decision making from the work, the jobs became so unattractive that close supervision was needed to ensure that, in Taylor's view, the inherently lazy man did not get away with "soldiering." When the manager assumed virtually all responsibility, the workingman didn't need to take any, as the role of each in the relationship complemented the other.

Twenty years after Taylor's rise to fame, another productivity experiment undercut his fundamental premise that reasonable men want to maximize their earnings. Researchers studying men wiring switching banks at Western Electric's Hawthorne Plant in Cicero, Illinois, found that production and earnings were consistently held to about two thirds of what was possible. When asked why they held back on their production, the men answered that they thought if they produced more, management would just lower the rate per piece.

When he extended the machine metaphor to workingmen, Taylor assumed that their minds were of no consequence. In fact, at one point he said, "I care not a whit for the thinking of the working man." Ironically, it was the men's thinking that caused Taylorism to fail. But his influence still permeates the way we work today. It is behind the way we design organizations, define jobs, measure performance, and incentivize. It's also behind the rising number of hours that we think we have to work and the nagging feeling that it's never enough. Carrying a BlackBerry and checking e-mail on Sunday are evidence that Drucker wasn't exaggerating Taylor's impact on the way we live.

THE FEEDBACK FALLACY

With its echoes of domination by the alpha and the damaging legacy of Taylorism, the relationship between a manager and an employee is challenging for both. The key to making it work, the conventional wisdom holds, is objective feedback on performance backed up by rewards and punishment. In effect, it's the only tool a manager has to shape behavior. In most corporations, regularly scheduled performance appraisals are conducted to provide such feedback and to ensure that the compensation of the employee is aligned with the objectives of the business.

But a landmark study at General Electric found that the company's performance appraisal system not only didn't work, it produced results that were virtually the opposite of what was intended. We readily accept that receiving information on how we're doing is the best way to improve our performance. It's built in to the way we raise our children, it's the purpose of the grading systems in schools, and it's behind the design of performance management systems in companies. But GE found that a manager's praise had no effect on performance one way or the other, while the areas that a manager criticized showed the least improvement.

Given how central feedback is to the role of the manager, one would expect that the publication of this study in the *Harvard*

Business Review would have revolutionized management. Yet forty years have gone by, and most managers are still giving feedback to their employees in the same old, ineffective way. It's as if the study never happened. When a manager's feedback fails, either it isn't noticed or the cause of the failure conveniently becomes an employee who is defective. Such is the way the mind works, and it's why our conventional management practices, logical as they appear to be, are doomed to fail.

This study also challenged the basic premise of behavioral science by showing that reward and punishment don't work the way we thought they did, but this wasn't the first time the behavioral science model was shown to be flawed. A decade earlier, the social psychologist Leon Festinger found in a simple experiment that reward produced the opposite effect of what was intended. The reason he discovered for this counterintuitive result explains not only why performance feedback fails, but why we don't notice the failure and why the conclusions of the GE study could go unheeded. At the same time, it gives us an incredibly effective management tool for the mental world we inhabit.

In the experiment, men were instructed to perform boring tasks for an hour. When they were finished, they were told that there were actually two groups involved in this experiment. The one they were in wasn't told anything before the experiment, but the other group had been briefed that the tasks would be enjoyable. The experimenter then asked the men to substitute for the person who usually did the briefing. The men were divided into two more groups: Those in one group would be paid a dollar for their participation and those in the other would receive twenty dollars. After they were done giving the briefing, the men were asked to rate how enjoyable the tasks really were.

The behaviorist model predicted that those receiving the larger reward would rate the tasks as more enjoyable, but the opposite turned out to be true. Those paid only a dollar rated the tasks as more enjoyable than those paid twenty dollars. Both groups of men were being asked to lie, to tell others that tasks they found boring were interesting. While twenty dollars was enough of a reward to justify the lie, apparently one dollar wasn't. The men who received the smaller reward experienced dissonance between their belief in their honesty and their willingness to lie about the tasks. Because this kind of internal contradiction is uncomfortable, they reduced the dissonance by convincing themselves that the tasks actually were enjoyable and that they weren't lying. Festinger called the effect *cognitive dissonance reduction*.

Given that we now know the mind creates our experience, it isn't surprising that the men would so easily change their view of the tasks. But at the time, this evidence of the power of the mind to change our reality was earth-shattering. It just didn't fit with either common sense or science. As the pioneering social psychologist Elliot Aronson put it, psychologists were forced to conclude that because "human beings think, they do not always behave in a mechanistic manner." But just as is the case today with research in neuroscience, this revolution in our understanding was largely ignored by those outside of the scientific community. It's too bad, because the theory of cognitive dissonance would have predicted the failure of GE's performance-appraisal system.

One way to understand how cognitive dissonance reduction works is to imagine how you feel when someone offers to give you feedback on your performance. The typical response is not, "Oh great, I'm going to have an opportunity to improve," along with a nice warm feeling. More often than not, the prospect of feedback is experienced with a sense of dread, particularly when it's coming from an alpha with a huge influence on one's career. If the feedback we receive conflicts with the self-image that we have spent a life-time honing, creating cognitive dissonance, it will be experienced as uncomfortable, and we will do what we can to eliminate the discomfort.

The most productive response would be for us to take the feed-back to heart, change our self-image from infallible to fallible, and work at learning a new way of behaving that incorporates the feedback. But this kind of change is the most difficult because of our deep-seated need to maintain our self-image. It's much easier for us to keep our self-image intact by rationalizing away the feedback, and either attributing the cause of the performance failure to external factors out of our control or discounting the source of the feedback. When the source is our bosses or people we don't especially care for, this is an attractive option. We question their ability to evaluate us, or their motivation.

The theory of cognitive dissonance also explains the failure of praise to improve performance, but it, too, requires that we incorporate mind into our view of why humans behave the way they do. In a study on reward, children were divided into two groups and given math puzzles to solve. In the first group, the children were rewarded for solving the puzzles. In the second group (the control), there were no rewards. The rewarded children initially did tend to spend more time on the puzzles. However, when the rewards were discontinued, they spent less time than they had before and less than the unrewarded group. This can be explained by drawing a distinction between intrinsic and extrinsic motivation. Intrinsic motivation comes from within—it is tied to our need for achievement and fueled by the neurotransmitter dopamine released by an area of the brain known as the nucleus accumbens. Extrinsic motivation, working for a reward, comes from outside of us—it is the motivation for the bonus at work, the compliments of people we care about, the treat we give our children for good behavior. The extrinsic motivation created by the rewards in the experiment led to a decrease of intrinsic motivation.

Because the reward was held out as the reason for the children to work on the puzzles, they saw it as the only reason. When the rewards were discontinued, they felt that there was no longer any reason to continue trying to solve the puzzles. The net result was that the reward had exactly the opposite effect of what was intended and of what we believe about rewards. Rather than motivating them to work on the puzzles over time, the use of the reward demotivated them. (This effect can be mitigated a bit by rewarding the performance rather than just the act of trying to solve the puzzles.) Since people are motivated intrinsically, the extrinsic reward of praise during the performance reviews at GE didn't motivate higher performance. People were already doing the best they could.

Punishment has also been shown to have an effect opposite of what we intend. In one experiment, two groups of children were placed in a room with some attractive toys. Each group was told not to play with the toys, but the first group received a mild threat of the consequences of disobedience while the second received a severe threat. Several weeks later the children were again placed in the room with the toys. Those who had received the mild threat were much less willing to play with the toys than those who received the severe threat. In the absence of a truly compelling reason, the children had convinced themselves that it was their decision not to play with the toys. Again, the strong extrinsic motivator decreased the intrinsic motivation.

These experiments demonstrate that in order to understand the effects of reward and punishment, including feedback that is experienced as either, we have to incorporate mind. It's not that we don't desire reward and dread punishment. It's just that how we view them is a result of everything else going on in our minds. Since extrinsic reward can make us feel that we have no other reason to do something, we might be better off rewarding behavior we want extinguished and then withdrawing the reward. Because punishment can make us more eager to do something, it makes sense to avoid using it.

MINDING BEHAVIOR

The effects of reward and punishment aren't as straightforward as we might've thought, and our need to reduce cognitive dissonance will determine how we respond to them. As Aronson put it, "Unlike rats and pigeons, human beings have a need to justify their past behavior, and this need leads them to thoughts and feelings, and behaviors that don't always fit into the neat categories of the behaviorist." In the physical world, reward and punishment are just what they are. In the mental world, they are what we think they are, adding a level of complexity to their use.

But it isn't only our reason that determines our response to rewards and punishment. Because the limbic system, which is responsible for our emotions, is much older and more deeply rooted in the brain than our newer prefrontal cortex, our feelings have a tendency to trump our reason. The sociologist George Homans believed it was our feelings that were responsible for reward and punishment producing the opposite of what was intended. While Frederick Taylor believed that a person's reaction to the prospect of a reward would be the result of a rational calculation, Homans recognized that it wasn't that simple.

He found that a reward is only effective if it's valued, but all too often, the one dispensing the reward gauges its value differently than the one receiving it. The boss may see a 5 percent salary increase as valuable, while the employee finds it so negligible that it's an insult and creates feelings of anger. Rather than being a motivating reward, it becomes a demotivating punishment. He also found that the value of a reward is a function of its frequency. With the very best of intentions, the boss may liberally reward people with praise, but rewards wear out with use as we become accustomed to them. The five hundredth time the boss praises the employee for a good job will not have the same effect as the first time. In fact, the employee very well may come to expect the praise and experience feelings of disappointment if it isn't forthcoming.

As Homans put it, "When a person's action does not receive the reward he expected, or receives punishment he did not expect, he will be angry; he becomes more likely to perform aggressive behavior, and the results of such behavior become more valuable to him." When unexpectedly we aren't rewarded or are punished, the amygdala kicks into gear, and we become aggressive toward the person responsible. Hurting that person is then experienced as rewarding to us.

The 5 percent salary increase the boss gives you when you're expecting 10 may be perceived as punishment and prompt aggression. The constructive criticism that you unexpectedly receive when you believe you are doing an acceptable job will also prompt aggression. It doesn't make any difference how the boss intended either, because in the mental world, what you believe something to be is what it is. Nor do you rationally calculate that 5 percent is better than nothing or that feedback is important for self-development. Instead, when you are being punished, it feels rewarding to punish in return. Ironically, it makes it rewarding to persist in the criticized behavior. This is what may have been responsible for the failure of criticism in the GE study.

Even beyond the aggression that punishment stimulates, its use is a problem for other reasons. If the behavior your manager would like extinguished has brought a reward, the punishment to prevent that behavior must be strong enough to overcome the lure of the reward. If the motivation is to avoid punishment, you won't necessarily refrain from the proscribed action. Instead, you'll just try to avoid being punished. If, as a child, you are punished for stealing candy, you are not necessarily going to stop stealing. Instead, you're going to work to avoid getting caught.

If getting less of a reward than we expect makes us angry, getting more makes us pleased. As Homans explains it, "When a person's action receives a reward he expected, especially a greater reward than he expected, or does not receive punishment he expected, he will be pleased; he becomes more likely to perform approving behavior, and the results of such behavior become more valuable to him." The first part of this is straightforward: Unexpected rewards have unique value. It is the second part that is counterintuitive: Punishment not delivered also has unique value. So when a person expects punishment, it is much more effective to withhold the punishment.

When I was a student at an inner-city high school in Detroit, I would on occasion sneak out of the building to smoke a cigarette. One day a teacher saw me and asked what I was doing. With the kind of logic only a teenager can come up with, I explained that I had come outside to smoke a cigarette since smoking was not allowed in school. The teacher informed me that I risked punishment. As I prepared to receive it, he told me that the next time I wanted to leave school, I should come to him and get a pass so that I wouldn't be punished. I was stunned. This incident didn't stop me from leaving school, but it did dramatically change my attitude toward that teacher. Hardly a motivated student up to that point, I started paying more attention in his class and worked hard to master the material.

It was a significant turning point in my life, and it eventually led me to become an educator myself.

In general, reward works to reinforce behavior when it is clearly paired with the desired behavior, when it is used sparingly, when it is valued, and when it is greater than expected. However, extrinsic reward, as we have seen, tends to diminish intrinsic motivation. While punishment may extinguish undesired behavior, it runs the risk of stimulating aggression, it must be quite strong to deter one from rewarding behavior, and it stimulates behavior to avoid the punishment. It appears to work best when it is expected, but withheld.

We like rewards and we don't like punishment. When we reward people or when we punish them, it appears to work. What we don't see is what goes on in the minds and hearts of the people we reward or punish. It is not immediately observable when our rewards diminish intrinsic motivation or when our punishment creates aggression. Nor can we tell how the person feels about us or what action they will take subsequently. This makes a manager's use of reward and punishment, and feedback that may be perceived as either, rather risky.

MANAGEMENT THAT WORKS
FOR THE EMPLOYEE

In light of the theory of cognitive dissonance, it's not surprising that the conclusions of the General Electric study have been ignored for forty years, because the study called into question the very role of a manager. Rather than accept that the premise behind management is wrong and have to sacrifice the alpha status that goes along with the role, it's much easier to just ignore the study's conclusions. After all, what we observe tends to confirm that reward and punishment work.

Reward and punishment are not intrinsically bad. It's their source that causes problems. As the cognitive paradigm predicts, it's the effects of the managerial relationship itself that produce counterintuitive results. When reward and punishment are dispensed by managers, employees are put in a subordinate role. In *Punished by Rewards,* Alfie Kohn makes a convincing case that all reward systems—whether at work, school, or in the family—are resisted because they are perceived as manipulative. As we've seen, the more responsibility a manager holds, the less an employee has to accept. When Taylor made managers the prime movers and gave them reward and punishment as their only tools, he pretty much ensured they would fail.

Given the overwhelming evidence that the managerial relationship as it's usually configured is self-defeating, managers should stop doing most of what they're doing today. Consider the following half dozen managerial practices:

1. Reward good performance as often as possible.
2. Punish poor performance.
3. Give timely feedback on performance problems.
4. Prescribe corrective action for performance problems.
5. Set measurable objectives.
6. Make an effort to closely supervise employees.

Each of these strike us as logically the right thing for managers to do, but they all fail in practice. We've already seen why reward, punishment, and feedback don't produce the results we intend or produce the opposite. But the same is the case for any action that puts the manager in a dominant role. When the manager prescribes corrective action, the employee does not have to take responsibility and has no motivation to make it work. The same is true of setting objectives. Plus, if employees don't meet the objectives the manager has set, they can claim they were too aggressive. People don't want to be closely supervised, and when they are, the managerial relationship quickly turns into a game of cat and mouse.

Since abstaining from these practices would seem like an abdication of responsibility, what should a manager do? Turn the tables and put as much responsibility on the employee as possible. Employees should set their own objectives, critique their own performance, and if there is a performance shortfall, determine what corrective action needs to be taken. When they are the ones responsible for their performance, the psychological dynamic of the relationship works for the manager, because the employee's self-esteem is positively correlated with their performance and the success of any corrective action.

The traditional role of a manager is Aristotelian, but it needs to become Socratic. Rather than tell employees what to do and create all of the negative relationship dynamics, the manager needs to ask. Rather than hand objectives to the employee, the manager should ask the employee to set them. Rather than give employees feedback on their performance, the manager should ask them how they think they're doing. Rather than tell the employees how to fix a problem, the manager should ask them what they think they should do to fix it. This is, of course, counterintuitive, for it turns the relationship upside down. As the prime mover of the organization, the employee now calls the shots and the manager is in a support role.

For the manager, this isn't an abdication of responsibility. In fact, it's a considerably more difficult way to manage. It's quick and easy to give an employee direct feedback, and there is a kind of pleasure to be derived from smacking a performance problem with some critical feedback. It takes more time and is more difficult to come up with a questioning strategy so that the employee self-critiques. For this kind of management to work, the manager must have patience and spend a good deal of time giving the employees the information required for them to self-manage.

Employees need to understand the dynamics of their industry and how their company is positioning itself. They need to be clear on the strategy and what kind of thinking and behaving is required to implement it. They should know specifically how what they do contributes to success or failure. But they also need real-time information about how the business is doing, and feedback on the success or failure of their efforts. It just can't come from the manager.

Instead, managers will need to install systems to provide employees with an objective source of feedback. This can be part of a goal-setting process in which performance against the metrics of the business is checked periodically, and it can include customer survey data and 360 degree feedback. Information on the overall performance of the business and any changes that might affect the employees can be provided by online systems that track the business, but some managers also make use of a periodic memo or newsletter.

Any reward or punishment employees earn should similarly be self-administered or dispensed by an objective system. As much as possible, the reward should approximate profit. There are many different ways to do this, but all link compensation to a set of objective measures tied to the performance of the business. Depending on the role, it may be production, sales, or customer satisfaction that is measured, or a combination to ensure the balance of activities needed for both short- and long-term success. Some businesses even use peer appraisals when there is no easy way to measure the quantity or quality of results. The measures can be individual, group, or both. So that there are no Prisoners' Dilemma dynamics, it shouldn't be the manager who evaluates the performance.

Regardless of how good the systems are, there will still be a need for human contact. Objective data is not a substitute either for the emotional connection that makes employees feel more committed to a business or for real-time, unplanned communication. Regularly scheduled one-on-one meetings will facilitate this kind of contact, but care should be taken that they don't appear as close supervision. An interesting alternative is scheduled office hours when employees are free to drop by if they want. Team meetings are a good way to build mutually supportive relationships and to ensure focus and alignment. Managers just need to be careful that they don't become an occasion for alpha displays.

This kind of participative management is not coddling or soft. It's just the opposite. When managers are setting objectives, giving feedback, prescribing corrective action, and dispensing punishment, it's harder for tough decisions to be made and acted upon. Few managers are eager to address performance problems head on. No one wants to cause distress to another person, and good managers will always question whether the objectives they set were achievable and the feedback they provided was fair. As a result, poor performance goes unchecked for far too long.

But when employees are setting the objectives and providing the feedback, the manager's self-doubt and emotion are removed from the equation. If the employees set the objectives and didn't achieve them, they should be held rigorously accountable. There is no reason why they should be sheltered from the competitive pressures the business is under. If corrective action doesn't work, their fate should be the same as that of a company which fails in the marketplace. Under this approach, tough performance management becomes much easier.

The new role of the manager, in the world according to neuroscience, is virtually the opposite of the old one. She doesn't order;

she asks. He doesn't set objectives; he provides the information to enable the employees to set their own objectives. She doesn't give feedback; she solicits self-feedback. He doesn't dispense rewards; he puts in place systems that self-administer. Employees don't work for her; she works for the employees.

It's like a tennis game: Whenever the employee tries to put the responsibility on the manager, the manager just sends it back over the net. But it takes self-awareness and discipline to pull this approach off. The manager has to guard against going for the expediency of telling rather than asking, and against the temptation of a periodic alpha display. The manager also has to understand the employee's version of reality to know how best to package communication and how to deal positively with any performance problems that can't be batted back. Finally, the manager must accept a relationship devoid of most of the perks that used to make the job so attractive.

REVERSING TAYLOR'S LEGACY

Taylorism is built into the design of most organizations that have been around for any length of time. It's in the structure, the control systems, and the job descriptions. But as we've seen, it's also in the managers thinking that they need to be in control: setting objectives, giving feedback, dispensing rewards and punishments. The first step for any manager who wants to improve performance is to recognize how the traditional role leads to suboptimization and self-defeat.

In newer organizations, particularly those in high technology, there is no legacy of structure, systems, and processes, so they have the luxury of "hardwiring" a different approach to management into their organizations. They can set up self-managed teams that use peer appraisals, install systems that help employees get feedback from the organization, and establish career managers to serve as advocates on compensation and promotional issues. Many believe such approaches are necessary to attract and retain younger, highly educated professionals. But the ultimate justification for them is that they lead to greater commitment, higher motivation, and better performance.

Perhaps what this new approach requires from management is clearest in traditional companies that have made the transition to a more employee-centric style, and there's no better example than Frederick Taylor's old employer, Bethlehem Steel. For the better part of the twentieth century, the company was one of the most successful in the United States. By the 1950s the company made so much money that eight of the ten highest paid executives in the world worked there, and it was said that if one blast furnace was needed, they would build two.

The line between the workers and the managers was clearly drawn by the company and reinforced by the union. Each mill had a country club built alongside it exclusively for management, and an office building well removed from the grit of the steel-making process. At the Sparrows Point Works in Maryland, there was a company town with streets designated by letters of the alphabet, and employees had to live on the street that corresponded to their rank in the hierarchy. In Bethlehem, Pennsylvania, workers lived on one side of the city and management on the other. There were different dining rooms in the headquarters building for different levels of the hierarchy, and they were furnished accordingly. It was even said that the high-level executives had shower priority at the country clubs.

But by the early eighties, foreign competition, substitute materials, and the mini-mills had transformed the industry, and the integrated steel makers were no longer profitable. One by one, Bethlehem's country clubs were sold off and the mills shut down. Still, Taylorism reigned supreme. The general manager of one of the divisions was pulled out of a training session on participative management by the president, who wanted to know why he was wasting company time and money on such things. At another division, a study team recommending cost-saving measures was told by the general manager that they had to earn the right to implement their ideas by first cutting costs.

The inefficiency of the company's approach to management was highlighted by a comparison with one of the mini-mills. With about the same revenues, Nucor employed seventeen people at its headquarters, while Bethlehem had over seven hundred. Nucor made steel at a cost of little more than one man hour per ton compared to Bethlehem's twelve. With the business dying and nothing left to lose, many in the company were willing to turn the traditional managerial relationship upside down.

At the Structural Products Division, a team of supervisors was given a free hand to redesign the business with my help. After a good deal of work, which included extensive research, site visits to cutting-edge companies, and in-depth planning sessions, their new organization was unveiled. They went from over four hundred professionals and managers to eighty professionals arranged in self-managed teams. Every phase of production was to be run by a dedicated team, and all decisions were to be made with the participation of those who would be affected, including the union. Even performance appraisals were to be done by the teams. Effectively, all supervision was done away with, and people were trusted to do the right thing.

The general manager and his executive staff redefined their roles to support the employees. They moved from the six-story headquarters building with closed offices, sitting outside the plant, to a one story metal building with an open bullpen in the center of the mill. For the first time in the history of the company, an all-hands meeting was held for both the union and management to discuss the changes, and information that used to be held close to the vest was shared widely, including financial results.

In the first year of operation after the changes, $85 million had been cut from expenses on revenues of $800 million. The second year's results matched the first, and the case was made for the division's new approach to management. It wasn't just that it was good for the people or that it was in line with the latest discoveries of neuroscience. It saved money, over $170 million in two years. Unfortunately, though, it wasn't enough. The business was still losing over $30 million a year, and the company could no longer afford the luxury of keeping the mill open, even though it had been the flagship plant. The decision was made to shut it down.

When I heard the news, I drove to Bethlehem to meet with the team I had worked with on the redesign of the division. At lunch with a supervisor who had been one of the most skeptical members of the team at the beginning of our work, I wondered aloud if there was anything we could've done differently. He told me that we had done the best we could, and that we'd succeeded in convincing other divisions of the company to adopt our approach. It just wasn't enough to overcome the drastic changes roiling the markets for structural steel. Then he added, "I've been here thirty-five years, but the last two have been the best of my career."

FROM CONTROL TO SUPPORT

Hierarchies and battles for control mark all primate communities, from chimpanzee bands in the wilds of the Gombe National Park

Primate Reserve to corporate organizations in glass and steel high rises. In the modern age, such relationships became even more difficult when the machine metaphor was extended to managerial relations. Add in behavioral science, with its disregard of mind, and the role of the manager became challenging at best and self-defeating at worst.

The only solution is for managers to stop thinking they can control behavior, whether through feedback or reward and punishment. Instead, they need to recognize that the process of natural selection holds inside a corporation as much as it does outside in the marketplace. People will behave the way they want, regardless of how rational we judge them to be. The best we can do as managers is to create an environment that selects for the behavior we desire.

As long as we remain in control, the relationship dynamic will work against us, driving our people either to passivity or outright aggression. This means the managerial relationship needs to be turned upside down, and for the manager it is going to feel like an abdication of responsibility. But it's not important what the manager feels, only what works. Rather than tell, we need to ask, when it comes to setting objectives, providing feedback, or deciding on corrective action. When the employee is the one responsible, the relationship dynamic is leveraged.

The role of the manager is now to provide the support and information the employee needs to self-manage. This can be built into the organization through design, like Bethlehem's self-managed teams. As Taylor's old employer demonstrated, when managers are eliminated, people step up and accept responsibility. Ultimately, though, it comes down to the willingness of the individual manager to consciously resist being in control. This creates an organization that is a better place to work and makes a lot more money.

FIVE

ORGANIZING LEVERAGE

Slime mold can teach us a lot about how to work together, perhaps because without brains they're incapable of Aristotelian logic. The species Acrasiales lives among the rotting leaves on the forest floor as individual organisms, ingesting bacteria they surround with their flesh. They're very prolific and reproduce every two or three hours, so the geometric growth in their population quickly exhausts the food supply in a given area. Then something quite unique happens.

One of the organisms, known as a founder, begins emitting a gas that attracts the others. They migrate toward it and form clumps, and then the clumps begin to move toward other clumps. Soon, the slime mold appears as streams of living matter, all moving in the same direction. The different streams ooze toward a central point, and a mound forms that grows upward into a stalk. When all the streams are incorporated, the stalk falls onto its side and becomes a slug about two millimeters in length. In this form, the Acrasiales make their way across the forest floor in search of an area where food is more plentiful. As the slug moves along, other individual organisms join up and become part of it.

When the slug reaches an area with more food, its migration stops and it again rises up in the shape of a stalk. The stalk grows taller and taller until a roundish ball of spores forms at the top. Once the stalk reaches a sufficient height, the spores are dispersed. As each lands on the forest floor, it opens and releases a new organism. And then the whole process begins again. The slime mold exist as individual organisms feeding on bacteria until the food supply is exhausted and they join together to search for more.

There are actually people who study such things; they're called animal sociologists, and they see slime mold as a metaphor for the ideal human organization. Each individual creature enjoys its independence until communal effort is needed to ensure an adequate food supply. The creatures then coalesce around leaders, forming small groups that merge into larger ones. Whether at the head of the slug or the rear, whether forming the base of the stalk or the spore mass at the tip, each one fulfills its role as an integral part of the whole. Each acts selflessly to ensure the release of new organisms from the spore mass.

The individual organisms don't chafe at their role as part of the slug. They don't envy those that form the head of the spore mass. The followers don't resent their leaders, nor do the leaders flaunt their power. Clumps don't compete with one another, sabotage the efforts of other clumps, or try to go their own way. All of their organized behavior happens without job descriptions, performance objectives, or incentive plans. Yet each tiny little creature plays its part perfectly. Although unfortunately named and oozing a trail of slime, they have it all over us when it comes to organized effort.

We battle for alpha status and don't care to be subordinate to anyone. We rate our success relative to others and envy those who we believe have a more privileged position. If there's more than one group, odds are there will be competition between them rather than collaboration. Truly selfless behavior is the exception. The organizations we create to run our businesses aren't very effective at fostering teamwork, nor do they tend to be warm and friendly places to work.

The enviable teamwork of slime mold is hardwired into its genes. A good percentage of our behavior is hardwired as well, but by what Richard Dawkins has called the selfish gene. We are in a competition for survival, and the winners get to pass on their genes. Although our sophisticated mental apparatus may appreciate the virtues of collaboration, it is no match for the instinct of self-preservation. We look out for number one. As one middle manager at a telecomm company put it, "if it comes down to a question of making my team successful or being able to send my son to college, it's a no-brainer."

Even when we buy into goals that require cooperative effort, it's just not in us to selflessly play the role of the stalk and support the spore mass. Nor are we eager to join a clump, and if we do, we don't want our clump to join together with others. Having evolved from hunter-gatherer bands, our orientation is still to the smaller, more immediate group. In his classic "Robbers Cave" experiment, Muzafer Sherif demonstrated how averse human beings are to being part of a larger group. Twenty-two boys were divided into two homogeneous groups, and separately transported to a camp at a state park in Oklahoma. Initially, the two groups were kept apart, but as soon as they learned of one another, each group wanted to run the other off. "These kids were not just playing at war. In a very short time, they had gone from name-calling to sticks and stones."

Our business organizations allow us to achieve goals not possible through individual effort, but attempts to get us to work together always butt up against the imperative of our genes. The challenge for all managers is to overcome first our selfishness and then our inclination to identify with the smaller, more immediate group. The conventional wisdom on how to accomplish this, just as in the case of management, is a product of our Aristotelian logic. As a result, virtually everything we do creates more problems than it solves.

Neuroscience offers us a better way to organize, but once again its insights will strike us as counterintuitive. Given our unconscious reduction of cognitive dissonance, our resistance to being controlled, and the hierarchical organization of neural networks, we'll get better results organizing to leverage people's natural inclination rather than attempting to thwart it. The hierarchy and functional specialization believed to be necessary in large organizations are eliminated, and in their place, a more natural process, not unlike how slime mold function, drives the focus and alignment required for organized effort. There's also a way to organize for group effort that dispenses with formal structure altogether. It leverages what we have that slime mold doesn't—a brain.

THE LOGIC OF ORGANIZATION

Most likely, the first attempt to achieve the benefits of large-scale collective action was in the military. A larger army confers an advantage, but only if it's an organized force and not a chaotic mob. As a practical matter, it isn't possible for a general to direct the activities of thousands of troops. There are just too many people following the conflicting imperatives of their selfish genes. At best, maybe he can effectively provide direction to ten people, and they in turn each can provide direction to ten more people for a total of a hundred. Each of these could then provide direction to ten more for a total of a thousand, and so on and so on. By creating a *hierarchy* of levels with a manageable *span of control*, a general could establish a *chain of command* to direct the activities of an army with as many soldiers as there are individual organisms in the Acrasiales slug.

This approach comes with its own set of problems. Whenever something is communicated through more than one person, it is subject to distortion, as we've all seen in the party game in which a message is whispered from person to person until it bears no resemblance to what it was originally. The further down the hierarchy the message travels, the greater the distortion. So to be effective, military organizations issue very precise orders with the stringent requirement that they be implemented exactly as directed. This requirement is backed up with the threat of Newtonian force, and not much independent thought or freedom of action is allowed. Well aware that their lives are at stake, most soldiers willingly accept the terms of their employment.

For most of history, armies were the only large organizations facing competition and requiring focused activity and tight management. By comparison, business enterprises remained quite small, at most made up of a handful of skilled craftsmen. But the industrial revolution changed all that when it brought about the *specialization of labor*. As Adam Smith described it in *The Wealth of Nations*, there are advantages to dividing the job of making pins into a series of discrete tasks assigned to different people. When someone performs the same job over and over, Smith explained, he learns from his experience to do it more efficiently, and productivity goes up exponentially. But when a job is broken down into its component parts, there is an even greater need for coordination, and the *functional organization* we're familiar with today evolved to provide it.

Even so, business organizations remained small enough to be easily managed until the middle of the nineteenth century. The average one employed no more than five hundred people and was usually located in a single mill building, or even on just one floor. In an organization of this size, it's possible for the manager to be close enough to the business to have relationships with all of his employees and to personally direct their work. When a business grew larger, though, the manager encountered the same problems as the general of an army.

This was precisely what happened with the railroads. There had never been anything like them before, and they put enormous demands on management. Given the need for a huge investment in rails and running stock, railroads had to be large to be economically viable, and by their very nature, their operations were geographically dispersed. Hands-on management wasn't possible, but tight control was even more of a necessity to ensure that a train running in one direction did not crash into a train traveling in the opposite direction. Passengers also expected a standard fee schedule and reasonably uniform treatment at any of the stations they might stop at.

The railroads quickly grew into huge business enterprises. By 1890, the Pennsylvania Railroad employed over one hundred thousand people, and all of its various activities had to be carefully synchronized. The only organizational models of sufficient scale to meet this challenge were from the military, and it was a young man named Harrington Emerson who brought them to the railroads. As a seventeen-year-old, he was present at the decisive defeat of the French by the famous Prussian general, Helmuth von Moltke. The general knew that while a large group of soldiers was an advantage in battle, it could be a disadvantage when it came to moving them into place or housing and feeding them. His solution was to organize them into smaller corps that could be combined into larger ones, and to make extensive use of staff to plan, refine, and standardize the operations of the army.

When Emerson later earned a degree in mechanical engineering and went to work for the railroads, he applied what he had learned from von Moltke. As a result of his work, all three features of the modern business organization were in place: hierarchy, a functional organization, and the use of staff to refine and standardize operations. In later years, Emerson became a colleague of Frederick Taylor's.

The railroads transformed local and regional markets into national ones, fueling the growth of the large companies we're familiar with today to serve them, such as Swift, Ford, AT&T, and U.S. Steel. They also became the organizational model for all others to copy, and their structure, systems, and practices were imported wholesale. But just like a metaphor extended too far, the military model, with its tight control backed up with Newtonian force, didn't necessarily fit businesses outside of the railroad industry. Relationship effects were inevitable when staff work replaced the thinking of the workers, and close supervision was required for employees who were seen as becoming increasingly lazy and passive.

The focus of this kind of organizational structure, with its carefully defined areas of responsibility and lines of authority, is on control, not on how work is done. As a result, legions of staff people and middle managers are required to ensure that organizational handoffs take place efficiently and nothing gets lost in translation. Still, given the tendency for different functions to take on an identity of their own and become fiefdoms, cooperation breaks down, and work moves haltingly through the organization.

The marketing function creates specifications for a product and passes them off to engineering. Engineering finds it can't design a product that meets all of the specifications, so it compromises on what it hands off to manufacturing. Manufacturing receives a design for a product too difficult to build, so it also makes changes. When the product is finally produced, marketing finds that it no longer meets the needs of the customer. Conflicts between the different functions must be shuttled up to the top of the hierarchy to be resolved, slow-ing down the process of getting a product to market and moving decision-making away from those who understand the issues best.

Making matters worse is that staff organizations find themselves in conflict with the line. Finance sees spending out of control while the line functions find themselves hamstrung by unrealistic bud-gets and controls. Human Resources is appalled at how people are treated, but the line sees HR programs as a needless intrusion. Pre-cious time and resources are invested in creating strategic plans that the functional managers put on a shelf and ignore. Potentially even more serious is that the line abdicates responsibility for the issues that are handled by staff.

While hierarchy, a functional structure, and the use of staff were all intended to solve problems resulting from the organization of large groups of people, they ended up creating even more. Neuro-science would argue that the cure is worse than the disease, but that neither is really necessary. The more structure we put in place, the more we go against the grain of human nature. Rather than attempt to counter our natural inclination, we should accept and leverage it. While the theory of evolution establishes our inherent selfishness, it also highlights our tendency to cooperate under certain circum-stances, and this tendency can be used to our advantage.

IT'S OUR NATURE

We're selfish, but not all the time. Under the right conditions, we want to be part of a group, as Solomon Asch demonstrated in his experiment on the human need to be accepted by others. He brought a subject into a group that was discussing whether line A or line B was longer. After listening for a few minutes, the subject was asked to give an opinion. In the initial trials, the group chose the line that was clearly and objectively longer, and the subject agreed with them. But then the group members, who were actually confederates of the experimenters, chose line B when line A was clearly longer. The great majority of the time, the subject agreed with the group on their choice. Moreover, the subject came to really believe that B was longer, as the conscious mind's need for group acceptance overcame the judgment of his or her senses.

Apparently, the desire to be part of a group has an evolutionary basis, just like our selfishness. Since our genes are only replicated through our offspring, the advantage of caring for them is clear. Those of us with children know viscerally how this works. We willingly put aside our interests for theirs. A good night's sleep, time for our own activities, and dinners at our favorite restaurants are displaced by nighttime feedings, interminable trips to the playspace, and happy meals. We don't need to learn how to be parents; we're hardwired to respond to our child's every little whim.

The evolutionary biologist William D. Hamilton argued that our *kin selection*, with its selfless behavior toward our children, gave rise to other altruistic behavior. When we lived in bands of hunter-gatherers, we would most likely have had some degree of relatedness to the other members of the band. Because we shared genes with them, we would be driven by our instincts to take actions for the good of the group. Once the value of cooperation with our close relatives was demonstrated, it would be extended to unrelated members of the band.

Cooperative hunting in bands would have produced a better result for our prehistoric ancestors than hunting individually. Sharing food among the members of the band would lead to the survival of a greater number than if one person hoarded a surplus while others starved. If all individuals called out a warning to the group whenever a predator was near, rather than simply fleeing and looking out for themselves, fewer would become prey. When we recognized the survival value of this *reciprocal altruism,* other social feelings and behaviors would also have been selected.

If we recreate the kind of group environment that gave rise to it, we can leverage our reciprocal altruism to encourage the cooperation we need in organizations. According to George Homans, the scientist who factored emotion into the use of reward and punishment, it doesn't take very much to do that. Homans studied all kinds of groups, from the workers who wired the switching banks at Western Electric to street gangs, and he found that the group dynamics in each were very similar. When he tracked the interaction of couples living in married student housing at MIT after the Second World War, he found that the main criterion for developing supportive relationships was proximity. Those who lived closest to one another and had the most interaction became friends.

This explains why functional specialists tend to coalesce into tight groups. With similar backgrounds and professional interests, they have enough in common to form friendships. Their day-to-day interaction, facilitated by their proximity, then causes them to identify with one another and form into a group. The Robbers Cave experiment showed us how quickly this can happen and to what lengths members can take their group identity. It also highlighted how to make smaller groups coalesce into larger ones. The counselors were able to get the campers to overcome their antipathy for one another by inventing an imaginary threat from a third group. In business, competitors are a ready-made common enemy.

The work of Asch, Sherif, and Hamilton shows us how to build focused, cooperative groups. Given the natural inclination to identify with a group and the need to be accepted, all managers have to do is create the environmental conditions where frequent interaction will lead to group identity. This will require physical proximity, a common threat such as competition, and a work group that doesn't exceed the size of a prehistoric band. When these conditions are met, cooperative behavior will naturally occur.

THE FREE-MARKET ORGANIZATION

Because our view of how to get people to cooperate is based on what's worked in the past, and because most of the time we're dealing with organizations that are already in existence, we keep thinking about how to solve problems that earlier solutions have created. Instead of worrying about how to get beyond hierarchy, a lack of cross-functional cooperation, and conflicts between line and staff, a better approach is to think about the best way of running a business with human beings who don't like being controlled and identify best with small groups.

That's exactly what the redesign team at Bethlehem Steel did. After a century of running their business with an organization modeled after the railroads they used to make track for, they decided to redesign it from the ground up. They wanted an organization that would support the implementation of their new strategy while facilitating the self-managed teams they were instituting.

Integrated steel mills like Bethlehem's were rendered obsolete by a simpler and cheaper technology. Rather than spend a billion dollars in capital for a facility to make steel from coke and iron ore, a mini-mill could melt scrap in an electric furnace that cost only about $150 million. This put Bethlehem at a huge cost disadvantage if steel was just a commodity to be purchased at the cheapest price. But the group of supervisors knew that their product wasn't just a commodity for all of their customers.

While some customers were only interested in the lowest price, others wanted the technical expertise Bethlehem had amassed during their century in business, and still others wanted custom payment terms, special shipping, and warehousing. The company's monolithic functional organization couldn't discriminate between these different customers nor deliver what they wanted. So three teams were put together to address the needs of these different customer groups. Each team was staffed with the people from all of the functions needed to make and deliver steel. It wasn't important who was in charge, for they were going to take their direction from the customer anyway. But in order for the groups to be manageable, they had to stay small.

Perhaps because they started with the needs of the business rather than the organization as it already existed, they created what organizational theorists would see today as a cutting-edge structure. Since it was focused on the customer, it was *market-oriented*. Because it facilitated the flow of work, it was *process-based*. With no one hung up on who was in charge and all decisions reached through consensus, it was a *self-managed team*. The steelworkers didn't know about organizational design, only about how to make and sell steel, so they didn't use any of these terms. They simply thought of their organization as the best and cheapest way to serve their customers.

There was just one problem. There was only one mill, and because it represented a huge capital investment, there was no way this asset could be duplicated for each market group. To produce an adequate return on investment, it needed to operate at full capacity, and long runs of commodity products were the best way to do that. This put its objectives in conflict with the two market groups that needed shorter runs of customized products.

For a time, the problem of the mill threatened to become a huge bottleneck that would sink the new organization, but then the group arrived at a solution that just seemed obvious. The mill should be looked at the same way customers viewed the company. It should operate as a separate business and structure its relationships with the market groups like those between a supplier and its customers. Each group would buy the services they needed from the mill and pay what was required. Short runs of customized products would cost more than long runs of commodity products, but that was acceptable because they would sell for more.

This structure did require a few more functional specialists so that one could be assigned to each group. But it eliminated all of the people needed to manage the hierarchy and the relationships between the functions. The net savings, as we've seen, were huge. By focusing on the market environment, by ensuring that key relationships were intragroup rather than intergroup, and by using market dynamics to manage those who couldn't be brought inside the groups, Bethlehem was able to eliminate hundreds of millions of dollars of inefficiencies and better serve its customers.

THE ENTREPRENEURIAL ORGANIZATION

Despite its innovations, Bethlehem's organization was relatively traditional. While it did leverage the natural inclination to be part of a group and minimized issues of control through self-managed teams, it still relied on salary tied to the achievement of objectives to motivate the right behavior, and we've seen the problems that can create. The supervisors were limited in what they could do because the Structural Products Division was part of a larger company. But their solution to the problem of the mill suggested that free-market dynamics could be used to manage all of the relationships in the business, not just those with the mill.

Such an organization, rather than having the invariable structure of a machine, would be a dynamic process more like natural selection. Focused on meeting the demands of the market environment better than the competition, it would be as purposeful as any organism in nature, with the selfish goal of maximum profit. Roles and relationships would evolve over time to meet any changes in the competitive environment. It would be made up of independent, entrepreneurial businesses, with customer-supplier relationships managed by market dynamics. The inside of the company would operate the same way as the external market.

Why shouldn't the relationships between "customers" and "suppliers" within a company be managed by a free market? The inherent conflicts between different functions, departments, and even individuals would then be resolved on the basis of money, just as in the example of the mill at Bethlehem Steel. We have a much kinder view of the gearheads in engineering, the slick willies in marketing, and the bean counters in finance, when they're our customers and paying us. We're also much more willing to put ourselves out when, rather than being compensated with a fixed salary, there's the prospect of being rewarded with profit.

In such an organization, all of us would run our own business, offering services at rates competitive in the market. If we did a good job and satisfied our customers, we'd flourish. If we didn't, our enterprise would go out of business. In areas where this wouldn't work because of the nature of the work or because the measurement systems would be too complicated, like production teams with highly interdependent jobs, we could create partnerships or small businesses. It wouldn't be necessary to implement the approach fully. Approximating the ideal would still bring benefits.

Free markets are highly efficient. Attempts to control them by imposing top-down structure create inefficiencies, as the decline of the Soviet Union and its planned economy illustrated. In the United States, the overregulation of airlines and telecommunications led to bloated costs and a lack of innovation. In both industries, deregulation brought both lower prices to the consumer and a host of new offerings. The Sarbanes-Oxley legislation passed in the wake of the Enron and Worldcom debacles has produced the unintended consequences of burdening companies with excessive costs for compliance, discouraging qualified people from joining boards of directors, and prompting an exodus of talent from public companies to private ones.

While the meltdown of the global financial system has its roots in a lack of regulation, no one is recommending doing away with the free markets that are the core of our economic system. If anything, the excesses in the subprime mortgage market are further evidence of how people will naturally pursue their self-interest and will be constantly on the lookout for loopholes in existing regulations. But while some degree of control will be necessary, we'll want to keep it to a minimum to avoid producing unintended consequences. The more we're able to align the pursuit of self-interest with the goals of the business, the less we'll need formal strictures to prevent inappropriate behavior.

Before the appearance of the large corporation, industries were made up of small businesses linked by customer-supplier relationships. When our country was founded, in the late eighteenth century, most American citizens were self-employed entrepreneurs. Small farmers raised sheep, and when it came time to harvest the wool, they hired independent shearers to remove the fleece. Spinners operating out of their homes turned the wool into thread, and weavers turned the thread into cloth. The cloth was cut and stitched into clothing by seamstresses, and the clothing was sold by retail merchants.

All of the people in the process were independent business-people. If their work was efficient and of high quality, they earned the reward of profit and were selected out by the competitive environment for future work and survival. There were no performance appraisals, strategic plans, or interminable management meetings. Thankfully, there were also no motivational seminars or management consultants. While spinning wool by candlelight or sewing for twelve hours a day to earn a living probably didn't lead to a great quality of life, at least there weren't any bosses to complain about.

There are still remnants of this approach today. The residential construction industry, with the exception of a handful of large companies, is comprised mainly of small entrepreneurial firms. A general contractor retails the project, oversees the process and schedule, and hires subcontractors to perform the bulk of the work. If they perform well, they get more work. If they don't, they have to find employment elsewhere.

Outsourcing today is in many ways a return to this model. The current trend is for a company to focus on its strategic advantage, where it can gain the maximum profit, and outsource everything else that would be a distraction. Even the monolithic domestic automobile industry has moved from Henry Ford's model of raw materials entering one side of the River Rouge factory and assembled cars leaving from the other. Component manufacturers now produce everything from brake systems to seats. There's even a firm that outsources innovation to Russian PhDs who lost their jobs when the Cold War ended.

In the 1920s, Alfred Sloan took what was then seen as the radical step of decentralizing General Motors and breaking it up into five companies with their own automobile brands, marketing, engineering, and manufacturing. The benefits Sloan gained, such as the market orientation that enabled GM to overtake Ford, would help make any organization more effective. Rather than limit decentralization to the top of the hierarchy, why not drive it down into the organization as far as possible? Modern information technology makes such "radical decentralization" much easier now than it was in Sloan's day.

Such an approach enables people to control their own destinies. From a Darwinian perspective, it's aligned with the urgings of our selfish genes. From a market perspective, it's more efficient and effective. From a cultural perspective, virtually every organizational innovation since the Western Electric Hawthorne studies has been aimed at fostering democracy and initiative in the workplace because it's good for both people and the business. Moving to an entrepreneurial organization is just the next step. While it may not be possible in all businesses and some control may still be necessary, it's worth shooting for.

CULTURE

Market-facing and process-based organizations can overcome the problems created by hierarchy and the functional groupings of specialists, especially when they're made up of small, self-managed teams. The entrepreneurial organization goes even farther toward eliminating cumbersome and inefficient structures by using market dynamics to manage key relationships. All of these innovations leverage natural selection as a better way to manage human activity.

But we have yet to incorporate the real insight of neuroscience—the dominant role of mind. Regardless of what structure, systems, and processes are used or how effective they are, it is impossible to prescribe how people should behave in every instance now and in the future. There are just too many variables, unpredictable changes, and ways to work around control systems. In fact, the more we attempt to prescribe what people do, the more we lose the advantage of the mind's ability to change how it works through learning. But given the primacy of mind in the mental world we inhabit, it's possible to control the behavior of a group without resorting to any structure whatsoever. All we need to do is shape the culture that shapes the thinking.

Culture is a convenient way of thinking about patterns of behavior in an organization that aren't hardwired by policies, procedures, or structure. Popularly, it has become a black box used to explain, in the absence of anything else, the failure of an organization to implement its strategy. The conventional wisdom, based on Aristotelian thinking, sees culture either as a thing or a set of observable behaviors. When Porter Goss took over the CIA, he attributed its intelligence failures to a "broken culture."

But in light of the mind's primary role in creating the world we inhabit, a better way of thinking about culture would be to see it as the mind-set of the organization. Because our mind-set is structured as a story, culture can be thought of as the collective story the members of an organization tell themselves, driving the way they perceive the world and act as a result. In the case of the CIA, the story wasn't aligned with the mission and goals of the organization.

If there has not been a conscious effort to shape the cultural story, the odds are that it will not be aligned with the organization's strategy. Since culture is collective and transmitted from person to person, it has continuity over time. When the strategy changes, the culture doesn't necessarily change with it. Even in a stable environment, without attention and careful orchestration, the culture evolves informally and can be at odds with the business. The men wiring switching banks for Western Electric created a culture that held back productivity. No matter how much structure is in place, it makes sense to consciously shape culture by managing how the organization's story is being told.

Research on the use of stories to further social movements suggests how this should be done. Sociologist Ronald Jacobs has studied such narratives and he believes that "Individuals depend on the existence of shared stories—or collective narratives—in order to express their sense of self. . . ." Successful movements, Jacobs has found, convince "people that the movement narrative coincides with their own personal narratives," and that their participation in the movement will further their individual goals. But they must "emphasize agency and ultimate success, rather than fate or ultimate failure," and they will need to do this more effectively "than other 'major' collective narratives."

As we've seen, the most effective stories are romantic, where the "heroes represent ideals and villains represent threats," and people are united "in the pursuit of a utopian future." In a corporation, people want the business to meet its goals for both rational and irrational reasons, but they also want to be part of something important and feel that their work is significant in a broader sense. When it's done well, the company's vision statement, the "happily ever after" of the cultural story, is the collective expression of this desire. It encourages people to move beyond a fair day's wage for a fair day's work.

When I started out in the corporate world, I worked for the computer manufacturer Digital Equipment Corporation. Because of the kind of work required to build large, expensive computer systems, the company had adopted the matrix organization of the aerospace industry, with most people reporting to both the manager of a business unit and the manager of a function. This hybrid structure aims for both customer focus and the advantages of a traditional functional organization.

Paradoxically, having two bosses gave employees more freedom to make decisions than having one boss, because it was up to them to resolve any conflicts between the two. This decision-making authority was reinforced by the company's founder, Ken Olsen, who was fond of saying, in contrast to the views of Taylor and Emerson, that no one knew as much about a job as the person doing it. It was up to each employee to determine what to do and how to do it.

This could certainly be a recipe for chaos, and there was a fair amount. It was also relatively easy to take advantage of the situation, and at one point I had a boss who lived on the coast and rarely showed up for work on nice beach days. But the company believed that whatever productivity was lost from these causes was more than made up for by the increase in commitment the culture encouraged. The company's incredible success, even when it employed well over one hundred thousand people, was evidence that this was the case.

The story the company told was on the order of the Arthurian quest for the Holy Grail. There were posters throughout the building that showed a photograph of the earth taken from outer space. At the top was the company name, and at the bottom was the line, "We change the way the world thinks." For me, this vision for the company was incredibly inspirational. Along with it came a set of stories, almost myths, about the Herculean efforts of people working to make the vision a reality, and the stories were true. In fact, people became so consumed by their jobs that the company produced a video cautioning employees to be careful about how much work they took on.

The corporate story was reinforced in every way possible. Ken Olsen sent out a memo once a month to all employees with his observations on the state of the company. Managers encouraged employees to "push back" and not just blindly follow the direction they gave. Work units were kept small and were distributed in two hundred facilities around the world, each designed to be like a college campus. There were no closed offices, even for executives. It's been twenty-five years since I left the company, but I still look back on my experience fondly. Although the company is today part of Hewlett-Packard, there's an active Digital alumni association, complete with newsletter.

The starting point for creating the cultural story is to determine precisely what kind of thinking and behavior is necessary for the company to implement its strategy. The story is then constructed with a plotline that pivots on how people change to overcome any obstacles in the way of achieving their vision of the future. It will describe precisely how people need to think and act, but at a high level. In line with Jacobs's research, the vision of the future should be aspirational and meet the needs of both the business and the individual.

The next step is to tell the story. Because the employees will create their version of it based on their total experience of the company, all of the details of the experience should be managed tightly. It should be conveyed in new-hire orientation, at training programs, and through all company communications. There should be a concise vision statement and regular updates on progress toward its accomplishment. Everything that can be orchestrated should be, from the behavior of managers to the physical environment.

Although our genes might be selfish, human beings know the value of cooperation, even when it requires a degree of self-sacrifice. We will work for the good of the group, especially if it enables us to achieve something we aspire to and can't accomplish on our own. The cultural story is how we can shape and leverage our natural inclination to be part of something bigger than ourselves. If we do it right, formal structure and control systems aren't even necessary.

GROUPS, MARKETS, AND MINDS

One can envy slime mold. It perfectly balances independence and collective effort. When the depletion of the food supply requires collective effort, the organisms coalesce to form first a slug and then a stalk with a spore mass on top. Each one willingly sacrifices itself for the good of the community and the next generation. No cumbersome organizational structures are necessary to control their behavior.

Human beings aren't so willing to sacrifice. We have evolved to be selfish and to look out for ourselves. Life is a zero-sum game and we're locked in competition for survival. Most organizational structures, systems, and processes try to thwart this natural inclination. Paradoxically, the hierarchy, functional specialization, and division into line and staff, created to ensure collective effort, end up producing just the opposite.

But by creating small groups physically co-located and by leveraging reciprocal altruism, our need to be accepted by the group, and the threat of competition, we can eliminate the barriers to collective action. In larger organizations, we can install market-oriented and process-based structures to create focus on the market and enhance workflow. We can go even further and make use of the process of natural selection that governs human activities by using free-market dynamics to manage customer and supplier relationships.

With structure or without structure, our greatest success will come from orchestrating how people think about their groups, by consciously shaping culture through a narrative. The most effective stories target our highest aspirations, are easy to identify with, and make it clear what people need to do to implement the business strategy. In fact, strategy should be the starting point for the design of any organization, and the kind of strategies the cognitive paradigm gives us, as we'll see, require the cooperation and commitment only a carefully managed culture can foster.

SIX

THINKING STRATEGICALLY

The war has gone on for nine years, and the advantage has swung back and forth. Then, just as victory seems to be within their grasp, a mysterious plague descends on the troops. A prophet proclaims the cause to be the abduction of a Trojan priestess by the Greek commander, Agamemnon. If the plague is to end, the seer explains, she must be returned to her father and a sacrifice made to the gods.

Agamemnon does not take this news well. Reluctantly, he agrees to send her back, but he then demands the priestess Achilles has taken in return. The great warrior takes the demand as an insult and goes for his sword. But just as he is about to make short work of his boss, the goddess Athena drops down from heaven and stops him. He obeys the goddess, but he then retires to his tent and refuses to continue fighting in the war.

This argument is the subject of the first story we have in the Western world, Homer's *Iliad*. Although these are two of the greatest heroes who have ever lived, the behavior of both can't help but strike us as childlike and self-defeating. Agamemnon alienates his best warrior and loses the advantage he brought the Greeks, while Achilles should have known that killing one's boss is never going to lead to good things, and his subsequent refusal to fight put both his comrades and his cause in jeopardy. Their behavior drives us to ask just what these men could've been thinking. The answer is nothing. They're not thinking at all. There's no thinking anywhere in the epic. There is no reflection, no deliberation, and no introspection.

Instead, our heroes act just like objects in the physical world governed by Newton's laws of motion. They go right at each other, letting force determine the outcome, and not just in this argument, but in the way they fight the war as well. There's no attack on the flank, no maneuvering, and no clever feints to mislead the Trojans. In fact, there's no strategy at all. Day after day for almost ten years, the Greeks just hammer on the Trojans and the Trojans hammer back. It's finally Odysseus who wins the war for the Greeks, not with superior force, but with strategy. The Trojan horse was his idea.

According to his plan, the Greeks left it on the beach as a sacrifice to the gods, and then sailed away. The Trojans debated whether or not to bring it into the city, but when sea serpents conveniently devoured those against the move, the horse was dragged inside the city walls. That night, Odysseus and an elite band of warriors hidden inside climbed out of the horse and opened the city gates to the returning Greek army. The rest is the history of the Western world, which may not have existed if it hadn't been for Odysseus.

He didn't go right at the Trojans and use force to breach the gates of the city, as Achilles had tried to do. Instead, he tricked the Trojans into opening the gates for him by presenting the wooden horse as something other than it was. This is the same way a metaphor works, and just as the old Yankee's pickle changed the thinking of the town's people, the sacrificial horse changed how the Trojans thought and acted. It wasn't Achilles' physical strength that won the Trojan War, but Odysseus' cleverness.

Whenever he found himself in a tight spot, Odysseus would work his way out of it by presenting himself as something other than he was, and the form this deception always took was a story. When he returned to Ithaca after his travels, he found a hundred suitors vying for his wife's hand. To trick the suitors into letting down their guard, he fabricated a story about himself as a blind beggar. Although he quickly became the butt of the suitors' jokes, enduring far worse insults than Achilles did, he never lost sight of his goal of revenge. When all of his preparations were completed and the time was right, he sprang his trap and made short work of the suitors.

In the person of Odysseus, the wisest of all men according to Zeus, Homer teaches the Western world how to think strategically. It is the same whether one is confronted with a hundred greedy suitors, an army of the finest warriors, or a one-eyed Cyclops. We focus on the long-term goal, formulate plans to achieve it, and calmly exercise self-control to ensure the plans are executed. Rather than directly challenge force with force, we leverage our resources by changing the thinking of our opponents so that they behave the way we need.

Our objective paradigm causes us to view conflict in terms of Newtonian force. Whether it's a one-on-one relationship, a military battle, or business competition, we see it as a contest where the strongest party wins. But because the world we inhabit is not physical but mental, the actions we take all too often have self-defeating relationship effects, and we don't avail ourselves of actions that would prove more effective because they strike us as illogical. When we view the conflict through the cognitive paradigm, though, we recognize how the nature of a relationship can be used to our advantage, how the environment can be a source of opportunity, and how the mind is the ultimate source of competitive advantage.

STRATEGY ISN'T LOGICAL

Imagine that I am a large manufacturer of automobiles, with huge fixed costs, excess capacity, and relatively low margins. My purpose is to maximize my revenues and profits for the quarter, because they determine how Wall Street values my company, affecting both the cost of capital for the business and my own compensation. From the law of supply and demand, I know that if I reduce my price, I will create a greater demand for my cars. I have data that allows me to calculate how much of a cut is needed to increase demand enough to raise total revenues and profitability. Based on my best logic, backed up by financial analysis, I cut my price a thousand dollars.

There is just one problem with this analysis—the market for automobiles is a web of relationships that includes customers and competitors. My behavior affects theirs, and theirs affects mine. My competitors, with access to the same data that I have and not wanting to see their products become less competitive, match my price cuts, and the supply and demand curves for the industry are shifted downward. With all of the companies now selling their cars at a lower price, I haven't gained any competitive advantage. My revenues are down and so are my profits.

But logic will object that this assumes constant demand, and total demand should increase with lower prices. While this is true at any given moment, it is not necessarily the case over time. The price cuts prompt a flurry of buying, until those who needed a car and those now able to afford one at the lower price have made their purchases. Having accomplished its purpose and helped to make the quarter, the price cut comes to an end and demand falls.

Logic obscures the interdependent relationships with competitors and customers, and it also prevents us from appreciating the role of the mind. Because the customers have minds, they are capable of using their past experiences to determine how best to act in the present. Observing the frequent bouts of price cutting in the automobile market over time, they learn not to buy until prices drop.

The ultimate effect of my logical price cut ends up being the opposite of what was intended. I have lower revenues and profits, and what's worse, a customer acclimated to waiting for price cuts. The quarter may have been made, but the unintended consequences stretch into the future. The next quarter will be even harder to make. Customers now waiting for the inevitable price cut will force the manufacturers to lower prices just to achieve the original level of demand.

Even with proprietary products and an absence of strong competitors, companies can still fall victim to relationship effects with their customers. Bausch & Lomb drove its managers with an annual goal of a 15 percent increase in both revenues and profits. As it posted quarter after quarter of these enviable results, its CEO was heralded in the business press as a visionary. After a while, however, when no more sales could be squeezed out of the market, it became clear that coercing managers with impossible goals wasn't quite as visionary as it might have appeared.

The company sold its products to distributors who then in turn sold to retailers. When the company was pressuring its managers to increase sales to the distributors by fifteen percent a year, it exceeded the capability of the market to absorb all of the product. With the aggressive goals hanging over their heads, the company's managers continually pushed the distributors to take more and more at the end of every quarter. Eventually, however, the distributors were so flooded with product that the only way to get them to buy more was to give generous discounts. Like automobile customers, the distributors had minds, so they quickly learned to delay their purchases for the quarter until the discounts were offered.

Soon, however, they held more product than they could do anything with and stopped buying all together. The unintended consequences were predictable—plummeting revenues and profits, and stressed-out managers. Creative accounting and fraud were next employed, but eventually the whole thing blew up with criminal indictments and a bankruptcy filing. Well before the cover stories in *Business Week* and *Fortune,* the CFO of one of the business units made an impassioned plea to simply accept missing a quarter. He was dismissed as naive.

Aristotelian logic distorted the view of both the automobile market and the distribution chain of Bausch & Lomb. As a result, actions intended to produce a certain result were actually producing the opposite. Because the cognitive paradigm focuses our attention on relationships, it enables us to anticipate such effects. When we factor in how the mind works, we're not only able to avoid falling victim to them, we're able to use them to our advantage.

THE SCIENCE AND ART OF STRATEGY

Clearly Odysseus was capable of a thought process that neither Achilles nor Agamemnon, nor for that matter the former CEO of Bausch & Lomb, were able to call upon. It seemed that he always knew just what to do to get the response he wanted from his opponents, and not only was he not surprised by relationship effects, he was able to use them to his advantage. Unfortunately, brain scans weren't available in ancient Greece, so we can't know for certain what was going on in his head, but we do have Homer's thoughts and the musings of a Princeton psychologist with an interest in both the classics and brain anatomy.

Julian Jaynes was an obscure researcher in the 1970s when he read about Roger Sperry's work with people suffering from epilepsy. Sperry had observed that seizures started as a burst of electrical activity in one region of the brain and then spread to others. Both hemispheres became involved when the electrical spikes traveled through the corpus callosum, the large bundle of nerves that connects the two hemispheres. Sperry's idea was to sever the corpus callosum and minimize the severity of the seizure by keeping it localized in one hemisphere.

To test his hypothesis, he performed his operation on fifteen patients. The results were stunning—the seizures stopped altogether. The only problem was that the patient literally became of two minds, and one didn't know what the other was doing. If a patient had his left eye covered and was presented with an apple, he could draw it but not name it. The reverse was true as well—an object viewed with the right eye covered could be named but not drawn. One patient was even observed pulling his pants up with one hand as he pushed them down with the other.

This anomaly led to the conclusion that the two hemispheres of the brain were specialized for different mental processes. Although it's not quite as simple as it first appeared, the left hemisphere of the brain, which controls the right side of the body, was seen to be the seat of our conscious reasoning. The right hemisphere, which controls the left side of the body, was believed to be where our emotions were located.

When Jaynes came across Sperry's research, he immediately thought of Achilles. The warrior was all emotion, and when reason made an appearance, it was in the form of Athena. The two cognitive processes were disconnected, just as they were in Sperry's patients, so Achilles experienced his reasoning as coming from the outside in the form of the goddess. Given that there are no references to conscious thinking in the *Iliad*, but an abundance of them in the *Odyssey*, Jaynes concluded that consciousness evolved in the period between the creation of the two epics.

The nature of this conscious thinking comes across in the way Athena convinces Achilles not to kill Agamemnon. She promises him a reward in the future worth three times what he was being asked to give up in the present. Freud called this *delayed gratification* and thought it was fundamentally how the conscious mind worked. He believed that it made possible the rise of agriculture, with its tilling of the soil and planting of seeds in the present for the promise of a crop in the future. Among her other duties, Athena was the protector of both agriculture and the civilization it gave rise to.

Today we do have brain scans, and they show that the nucleus accumbens, which we have seen is responsible for feelings of pleasure, matures before the orbital frontal cortex, which is the location of our faculty for long-term planning. The different rates of maturation of these two areas, in the view of Gary Marcus, explains why teenagers are "pathologically driven by short-term rewards." Odysseus, on the other hand, appeared to have a rather well-developed orbital frontal cortex.

So why do automobile executives and the former CEO of Bausch & Lomb fail to adequately anticipate the long-term consequences of their actions? Damasio's experiment with the decks of cards offers a hint. In the world of Aristotelian logic, we discount emotion in favor of objective reasoning. The right hemisphere of the brain, which is responsible for emotion, is also responsible for seeing wholes. This big-picture perspective recognizes that making the quarterly numbers is just a small part of running a successful business and can't be pursued at the expense of the longer term. When we discount emotion, we lose access to the big picture. It isn't as much a question of emotion *or* reason as it is using the two in tandem.

The night before Odysseus is to execute his plan to slaughter his wife's suitors, he is awakened by the laughter of his wife's maids cavorting with the suitors. He's tempted to make short work of them, "torn in thought, debating, head and heart." But in contrast to Achilles' need for the goddess of wisdom to control his emotions, he is the one who recognizes that it would jeopardize his longer-term goal. So he controls his desire for immediate gratification with the words, "Bear up old heart! You've borne worse, far worse. . . ." Signals were flowing freely through Odysseus' corpus callosum.

The execution of strategy requires delaying the gratification of our short-term emotional wants, but not at the expense of the insight emotion brings us. Perhaps the pendulum has swung too far, and we now favor our left hemisphere over our right more than we should. But we can bring that hemisphere back into play by consciously attending to the two aspects of our experience highlighted by our awareness of the big picture, relationships and the environment, and the cognitive paradigm enables us to do that. To keep our focus, we can coach ourselves as Odysseus did, or we can just tell ourselves a story.

LEVERAGING THE ENVIRONMENT AND THE MIND

Before there were corporations that needed to mobilize large numbers of people in pursuit of a common goal, there were armies facing the same challenge. The military established the pattern for how large business organizations are built and managed, and in fact the word strategy comes from the Greek *strategia,* meaning generalship. So if we want to understand how best to formulate a competitive strategy, the battle plan is not a bad place to start. One of the best examples is Henry V's classic battle against the French in 1415. It teaches us how to leverage both the environment and the minds of our competitors.

Henry had sailed to France to assert his claim to lands his grandfather had won. His first battle ended in victory, but it took longer, consumed more resources, and cost more men than he had anticipated. In his weakened condition, he decided to avoid any more battles, and just march symbolically up the coast to Calais and sail back to England. The night before he was to arrive there, he found himself on the edge of a newly plowed field near the small town of Agincourt. There, across the field, he saw the entire French army, outnumbering the English by twenty to one. They were fresh, well armed, and eager to claim the glory they felt they were due. The English were worn-out, homesick, and convinced they'd be defeated in the coming battle.

That night as he wandered among his dispirited troops, the king could hear the French feasting across the field, raising toasts to the victory they were sure to win the next day. In almost all traditional warfare, and business competition as well, victory favors the stronger force. Henry's only hope for survival was to come up with a plan that would turn the French advantage in numbers into a weakness. At some point during the night, looking out across the field and listening to the detested French, he figured out just how to do it.

The newly plowed field was muddy, and narrower on the English side than on the French. Henry had his men drive stakes into the ground on his side of the field at a height that would impale a charging horse, and he placed his infantry in front of them so that the stakes would be hidden from view. On the sides of the field, he deployed his archers with their longbows. Although the conventional wisdom held that Henry should've been in a defensive posture, his troops were deceptively arrayed as if for an attack.

When morning came, Henry spoke some final words to his troops and then launched the attack by signaling his archers to fire their arrows. Given their distance from the French, the arrows did no physical damage, but they infuriated the French leadership. Quickly, they mounted their horses and started galloping full speed down the field toward the English. But when they reached the narrower end of the field, there was no room for all of them. At just that moment, the English infantry stepped out of the way and exposed the stakes. The French were trapped with nowhere to go, and they were easy targets for the archers, who began raining arrows down on them. Nor was a retreat possible, for wave after wave of cavalry followed the leadership in quick succession down the field.

The French who didn't fall victim to the arrows were either driven into the stakes or trampled by their own cavalry. By the end of the battle, there were over six thousand French casualties, while the English lost only about a hundred men. Recognizing that he might need the French as allies in the future, Henry made a point of treating his captives graciously and later cemented an alliance with them by marrying the French king's daughter.

Conveniently for our purposes, Henry attended to all of the elements one must consider for a successful strategy and made the most of them. He analyzed the environment that he would be fighting in and recognized that it could be used to his advantage. The horses would find it difficult to get their footing on the muddy field, and the French cavalry would be too crowded together to fight when they reached the narrower English side of the field. He factored in the French mind-set of superiority and arrogance, anticipating that they would race down the field to his trap when his archers fired arrows at them.

In the spirit of Odysseus, Henry tricked the French by hiding the stakes blocking the end of the field and having his archers act as if they actually were attacking. This strategy intensified the competitive dynamic of the relationship, which worked to Henry's advantage and enabled him to change the greater numbers of the French into a weakness. Finally, he thought beyond his immediate goal of survival to strike an alliance with the French that might prove useful in the future. The best strategists anticipate the reactions to their moves and constantly ask, "What's going to happen next?"

BUSINESS STRATEGY

Because its roots are in the military, it's easy to think of business strategy as some sort of competitive shoot-out. After all, the competition is the enemy and the goal is to defeat the enemy. But this is extending the military metaphor too far. The difference between military strategy and business is the presence of a third party, the customer. The goal of the strategy is not to defeat the competition in a head-to-head battle, but to *meet the needs and wants of the customer better than the competition*. When it becomes just competitor against competitor, we get caught up in the relationship effects and lose sight of the customer, as we see when competition is focused on the single dimension of price cuts in the automobile industry.

As would be expected, given that free markets are Darwinian, the cognitive paradigm captures the nature of business competition better than the objective one. While species compete to meet the demands of the natural environment, companies compete to meet the demands of the market environment, and that is made up of customers. The big difference is that while the natural environment is dumb, customers have minds that shape their demands.

Just as in autos, the airlines are addicted to price wars, with the same disappointing results. One company that figured out how to move beyond the destructive head-to-head competition was People Express. Don Burr, the founder and CEO, came up with a strategy that although based on price, leveraged the changes in the environment and addressed the mind-set of the customers in a way that couldn't be matched by the competition.

In late 1979, when People Express was founded, the country was still suffering from the fuel shocks of the seventies. The skyrocketing cost of oil had caused the economy to stagnate, and it hit the airlines even harder than most industries because jet fuel was their largest expense. Since the price had gone up dramatically in a very short period of time, there had been no opportunity to drive efficiencies, and most carriers were flying planes that were highly fuel inefficient.

Besides, the airlines had been regulated and were used to the peaceful coexistence that kept both costs and prices high. That era had just come to an end with President Carter's signing of critical legislation deregulating the industry. Socially, the country had not yet entered the "Me" decade of the 1980s, and there was a strong populist ethic. With the hostage crisis dragging on in Iran, it felt as if the American ideal of democracy was under fire.

Most airline customers were either businesspeople flying on their company's dollar or relatively well-off private passengers, and both groups were largely price insensitive. However, there was a large group of potential customers who would consider flying as an alternative to driving or taking the bus, if they could do so for a reasonable price. These were the customers People Express decided to go after.

People Express's competitors were established carriers, and their strengths and weaknesses were just what you would expect from companies in a regulated environment. They knew their business and had the necessary plant, processes, and people in place to run them. They had established relationships with their suppliers, shareholders, and banks, and they had name recognition with customers. This gave them forward momentum.

However, because the industry had been regulated, they were complacent and invested in maintaining the status quo. The conduct of their business had become routinized. Standard operating procedures were in place, and corresponding neural networks had been embedded. They had high costs and were slow to innovate. Having become accustomed to a market in which selling just seats was sufficient, they didn't necessarily understand the wants of their customers or how to address them. If they thought about them at all, they would have most likely defined them with Aristotelian logic as more comfortable seats and fancier meals.

In contrast, as the new kids on the block, People had nothing in place to run an airline and everything had to be created from scratch. While this put them at a cost disadvantage on the experience curve, they also benefitted from the absence of legacy costs and practices. They didn't have a high-priced workforce with expensive pension obligations, entrenched processes that weren't efficient, or costly facilities. While most organizations and cultures evolve willy-nilly and aren't necessarily configured to implement the current strategy, People Express had the luxury to design their organization specifically for the implementation of their strategy.

Plus, they had Don Burr as their CEO. He was an experienced airline executive, having run Texas Air in the seventies under the legendary Frank Lorenzo, who went on to turn the old Eastern Airlines into the world's largest carrier. Burr knew both the strategic and the operational side of the business, and had the contacts to assemble a high-quality management team. Because he had worked on Wall Street, he was able to raise the kind of money needed to start and grow the airline. He understood what deregulation would do to the industry and how to take advantage of it. He was also charismatic enough to pump up a room full of investment bankers or maintenance workers, as the need might be.

There's no logical algorithm to follow to come up with a competitive strategy, no syllogisms or laws of logic that can be applied. But having considered the nature of the competitive environment, the needs and wants of the customers, the competitors' strengths and weaknesses, and our own, a neural network is embedded in our brains that will select out a strategy in harmony with it.

Such a strategy, just as in the case of the battle at Agincourt, must leverage our strengths relative to the competitors' to create an offering that will better satisfy the demands of the market environment. We can get a bit more direction if we make use of our theory of mind and think about our offering from the customer's perspective. There are only two reasons people buy a product or a service. Either the offering is cheaper or it's better. Cheaper is straightforward, and clearly that was People's dominant strategy.

The company gave up the established market of traditional flyers and took advantage of deregulation to go after the untapped price-sensitive market with a low-cost offering. Because they were not burdened with fuel-inefficient airplanes or legacy costs and practices, they could price their offering so that it was competitive with driving or taking a bus. Given their lower cost structure, they had an immediate competitive advantage over the established carriers. As a start-up, they were small enough not to be much of a threat anyway.

A purely low-cost strategy will only work for a while; eventually either existing companies or new entrants to the market will duplicate it. But if the company can differentiate its offering at a minimal incremental cost and not undercut its low-cost strategy, it can more effectively attract and hold on to its customers. It can then fend off any competitive attacks based solely on price.

Another way of thinking about it is that meeting the customers' basic needs is just the ante that gets you in the game. The real advantage comes from going beyond what customers need to what they want. In the world according to neuroscience, the key differentiator is going to be mental, not physical. While it isn't always obvious what customers want, the more we understand the story they're telling themselves, the better we'll be at discovering and addressing what motivates their buying decisions. There may be individual variations, but the overriding story will be a masterplot of our culture.

Don Burr realized that the masterplot foremost in the minds of his target market was the story of American democracy, "We the people" coming together to build a "more perfect Union." This is deeply rooted, and taps into those high-level ideas that we've seen drive much of our behavior and thinking at lower levels. People Express leveraged this story both inside and outside the company with its people-centered organization, employee ownership, and name. Customers weren't just buying a seat, they were voting for democracy and the American way.

This not only created a buzz for the airline, it made customers more willing to accept the long lines and waits in the Newark North Terminal that occurred all too frequently. It also made it easier to attract the kind of employees who were willing to work for a lower wage plus stock, enabling the company to keep operating costs down. In the mental world, a seat is not just a seat and a job is not just a job. They are what we believe them to be, and that is a function of the story we tell. People Express told a great story, and it changed the competitive dynamic of the marketplace.

Brilliant as any strategy may be in concept, it isn't enough to ensure success. More companies fail because their strategy isn't implemented than because it isn't robust enough. The relationship between the formulation and implementation of the strategy doesn't receive the attention it should, both because of our Aristotelian logic and because those formulating the strategy usually aren't the ones who will implement it. But every aspect of People's organization was designed to operate just like natural selection, both to keep costs down and capitalize on the populist theme.

In place of the hierarchical management and standard operating procedures of the established carriers, People Express used self-managed teams that determined their own work processes. In place of rigid job descriptions, enforced by the established carriers' unions, the airline had the flexibility to rotate people through different jobs. Rather than fixed salaries, stock ownership aligned with profitability made up the bulk of compensation. The aspirational mission of showing the world how to run a business democratically took people beyond a fair day's work for a fair day's wage. As a result, operating costs were low, morale high, and customers satisfied with a "unique" flying experience. By 1984, People Express had become not just the fastest growing airline, but the fastest growing business ever.

THE MIND OF THE STRATEGIST

Within six months, though, People Express was bankrupt. Given the high profile of the company and its success in implementing so many of the management practices that would later become fixtures of companies like Apple and Google, there's been a lot of speculation about what caused its demise. Some were quick to fault its wide-open organization and employee-centric policies. Others believed the airline just grew too big for the established carriers to ignore, and their deeper pockets enabled them to win the ensuing price-cutting battle. Don Burr attributed the cause to the rise of yield management software, which enabled the airlines to adjust prices on individual seats in response to demand.

But an experiment called the Stanford Marshmallow Test suggests that the reason for People Express's failure can be found in the orbital frontal cortex of Burr's brain, the same area Gary Marcus believes is responsible for the high-risk decisions of teenagers when it's underdeveloped. Four-year-olds were placed in a room with a one-way mirror and a marshmallow on the table in front of them, and they were given a choice. They could eat the marshmallow right away, or if they waited twenty minutes for the researcher to leave and come back, they could have two marshmallows.

Given the impetuousness of four-year-olds, the results are not surprising. About a third ate the marshmallow right away, a third tried to wait but couldn't make it, and a third waited the full twenty minutes for the researcher to return. But what the researchers learned when they revisited these kids fourteen years later is surprising. Those who were willing to wait the twenty minutes for the other marshmallow tested on average over two hundred points higher on the Scholastic Aptitude Tests. The four-year-olds are now in their forties, and follow-up research has found that they are also more popular, have had greater career success, and score significantly higher on intelligence tests. They have proven to be great strategists. The ability to make the decision to delay immediate gratification for the promise of greater gratification in the future pays huge dividends.

There was one critical decision Burr made that led directly to People Express's bankruptcy filing, and it seems to have been made without any input from the orbital frontal cortex. By the end of 1984, the company was growing quickly, but not quickly enough for Burr. He became convinced they should move beyond a regional focus and go national. Given the hub-and-spoke model of the industry, this meant a western hub was needed in addition to the eastern one in Newark. But rather than sticking to the strategy that had brought them success and build it from scratch, Burr went searching for an acquisition.

When a carrier named Frontier Airlines in Denver became available, he decided to buy it. In itself, this was a questionable move. Anyone who's worked on Wall Street, as Burr had, knows that fewer than one third of acquisitions are successful. Even more of a concern was that the key to the company's competitive advantage was innovative human-resource practices and procedures that were not going to work at an established carrier, let alone a unionized one like Frontier.

But perhaps most curious was how the acquisition took place. Burr was experienced enough in the financial world to understand the need to calculate the highest price he could pay for Frontier and not go over it, but he ended up going way over it. The acquisition sank People Express, which became loaded with debt and unable to implement the kind of cost-saving measures that had proven so successful. Why did Burr pay more than he should have? Because there was another bidder for the company and his name was Frank Lorenzo.

It's open to debate whether Burr's former boss actually wanted the airline, or just wanted to drive the price up so high that it would bankrupt Burr. Apparently, there was a bit of bad blood between the two because when Burr left Texas Air to found People, he took the whole executive team with him, including Lorenzo's personal secretary. One can't help feeling that Burr's desire to beat out his former boss got in the way of his business sense. In any case, Lorenzo played the competitive game to the hilt and let Burr bankrupt himself. When People Express ran into financial trouble, Lorenzo picked up its assets at a fire-sale price.

In retrospect, one can't help wondering why Burr went after an airline that didn't fit his strategy and paid far more for it than he should have. But anyone who has ever been involved in an acquisition has felt the thrill of the hunt, and the bidding war with Lorenzo can't help but recall a similar competitive escalation that occurred three thousand years earlier between Achilles and Agamemnon. Just like a teenager, Burr became involved in the emotions of the moment and lost the long-term perspective the orbital frontal cortex offers.

According to the *Iliad*, the battle against the tug of immediate gratification is a story as old as our culture, but we're not doomed to lose it. Researchers have found that performance on the Stanford Marshmallow Test improves when children stop thinking about the marshmallow as "yummy and chewy," and start thinking about it as being like a "cloud." This is just like the cognitive reappraisal we saw change the emotional response to the picture of the woman crying. It does appear that people can train themselves to be better at delaying gratification.

Psychologist Jeremy Gray thinks the best way to avoid falling for the lure of immediate gratification is to clearly envision the future, and this approach is tailor-made for ensuring that strategies are implemented. Even if we were capable of remaining reasonable in the face of emotional temptations, there are just too many decisions to be made for our logic to handle. Instead of being driven by our conscious reasoning, implementation should be driven by the story with the vision of the future we tell ourselves. It's the only way to ensure that all of our decisions and actions are in sync and that we're not being distracted by the activity of the nucleus accumbens.

The more we tell the story, the more it's embedded in a neural network, and the more comprehensively it drives our thoughts and actions. But the story will only work if we really believe it. As a discipline, every one of our decisions should be checked against it, just as Odysseus checked his desire to murder his wife's maids. Perhaps People Express would still be in business today if Burr had had the benefit of the latest research in neuroscience and exercised a little bit of Odysseus' knack for telling a story and sticking to it. Then maybe he would have opted for slower and more reliable organic growth. That's been Southwest Airlines' strategy and they have now become the most successful airline ever.

THE COUNTERINTUITIVE STRATEGIST

Odysseus' strategy changed the wooden horse from a siege engine into a sacrifice to the gods. Henry's strategy changed the French strength of greater numbers into a weakness. Don Burr's strategy changed an airline seat into a vote for the American way. In each case, the strategy changed how people thought in counterintuitive ways, so that the nature of the competition wasn't just force against force. In the mid-1990s, a small high-technology start-up named Cambridge Technology Partners revolutionized the information technology services industry by taking a counterintuitive approach to the formulation of strategy itself.

When I first interviewed the CEO, I learned that he'd never attended college or business school, with the exception of an executive education program. Instead, Jim Sims left high school to join the Navy, where he was trained as a computer technician. After the service, he went right to work for a computer manufacturer. He was so charismatic and such a natural salesman that he quickly rose to the top and became a sought-after CEO. When venture capitalists were looking for a leader for an interesting high-tech start-up, Jim seemed like the ideal candidate. By the time I became his consultant, he had already taken the company from just under ten to over a hundred million dollars in revenue.

I was puzzled by how this guy became such a consummate

businessman without the requisite formal training, so I asked him one day. He explained it by describing his years selling newspapers on a street corner in Detroit. "A bunch of us used to stand on a street corner at a stoplight. When the light changed red, everybody would run to the cars at the front of the line, but I would run to the cars further back where there was no competiton.

"You know, the papers used to cost seven cents. Now, most people would ask for a paper, give me a dime, and tell me to keep the change. The margin wasn't bad, but the real opportunity was the people that gave you a quarter. As if looking for their change, I would take off my gloves one finger at a time and then start searching all of my pockets. I would just keep them waiting until the light changed and people started honking. Then they'd tell me to keep the change and would drive off." Early on, Jim had learned to go where the competiton wasn't and to anticipate and leverage the responses of his customers.

CTP was in the business of developing applications using client-server technology. This industry was virtually locked up by the technology consulting divisions of the then Big Six accounting firms. These firms already had relationships with the finance departments of most large corporations, so it was easy for them to cross-sell information technology services. Newcomers to the market had little chance of getting a hearing, let alone a contract.

All of this changed because of a brilliant MIT professor with a flair for the theatrical. He held seminars for chief information officers to introduce them to the latest client-server technology and graphic user interfaces. At night, he would have his graduate students dummy-up screens so that the CIOs could experience what a custom-designed application using the technology could do for their businesses. They were so impressed that they immediately wanted to hire the professor to build the applications. He had started CTP to meet the demand for these services. When the company ran into problems, the venture capitalists took it over, and brought Jim in to run it.

With offices located in Cambridge, midway between Harvard and MIT, Jim was quickly able to build a talented staff. With his sales expertise and the staff's knowledge of the technology, they set about reinventing the business. Rather than formulate strategy by starting with customer needs the way People Express did, they went at it counterintuitively. They started with the customer's frustrations and dislikes, and then designed an offering that would eliminate them. This one change then led to a completely different approach to all aspects of the business.

The biggest dislike in application development has always been projects that run over time and budget. It makes it impossible for CIOs to plan and effectively manage their business. Worse yet, such projects destroy their credibility with the line. To eliminate this source of frustration, CTP decided to offer guaranteed fixed-time, fixed-price contracts. The company knew that this strategy couldn't be easily matched by the competition because all of their systems, including compensation, were based on billing for time and materials. To match CTP's offering, they would have to completely redesign their businesses, and the cost and time involved would be prohibitive.

To make this one change work, others were needed. For the company to guarantee a fixed time and a fixed price, they had to eliminate change orders and midcourse corrections. Standard practice in the industry was for the client to give the vendor the specifications for the application, and inevitably this handoff would lead to misinterpretations, which then would require adjustments. The way around this was for the client and vendor to create the specifications together. CTP's approach was to form a team made up of representatives from both who would spend a week working together to create the specifications.

But this was an expensive proposition, so it led to other changes. CTP turned what had been a service into a product by putting a fixed price on the process of creating the specifications. To make sure the team used their time effectively, they staffed each project with a trained facilitator, and this allowed them to address another key frustration. Most development projects focused only on the technology, and inevitably there would be behavioral issues when it came time for implementation. With the participation of the facilitators, these issues were identified and addressed up front.

There is always friction in the relationship between the consultants and the clients, particularly when it comes to sales, but the team approach prevented it from occurring. In other firms, the vendor would sit across from the client and pitch their services, but at CTP there was no pitch to sell services. Instead, at the end of the week-long workshop to develop the specifications, the CIO would come in for a presentation given by his people on what the application should look like. Effectively, the CIO's own people were the ones selling him on the application. Not only had Jim changed a service sell into a product sell with a fixed price, he had the client selling himself.

One simple shift, from meeting needs to eliminating frustrations, led to a counterintuitive habit of mind, an idea lodged at a high level, which was then brought to bear on all aspects of the business, even turning problems into opportunities. Since the company was growing so quickly, it was forced to hire a number of young developers right out of school. Given the business model, these people were in front of the client from day one, in contrast to the established industry practice of having only senior people meet with the client. The necessity quickly was recast as a virtue. As the president described it to me, "Initially we were concerned how clients would respond, but we just stressed how much fun it was to work with young, bright, energetic people. After a while, they saw them that way too."

ENVIRONMENT, RELATIONSHIPS, AND MIND

Strategic thinking is fundamentally how the conscious mind works, and most likely it was an adaptation that evolved to address human conflict. We stand back, decide what we want for the future, and arrange our activities in the present to achieve it. It's basically the same thought process whether we're up against a monster with a taste for human flesh, suitors who are after our spouse, or an army we'd like to defeat. Given the mental Darwinian world we compete in, we attend to the environment, relationships, and mind.

The big difference between strategy in human conflict and in business is the presence of the customer. Our goal is not to focus on defeating the competition, because the relationship effects will only pull us into a destructive downward spiral, but to meet the needs and wants of the customers better than they do. When we consider the environment, the customer, and the competition's strengths and weaknesses relative to our own, we prime the mind to come up with a sustainable competitive strategy that ensures we'll be either better or cheaper.

Ultimately, though, in a mental world, the real competitive battle is going to be fought in the mind. By addressing the way people think, we can move beyond the battle of force against force that typifies competition in the Newtonian world. The place to start is with the stories people tell themselves. The more we understand what they are, the better we'll be at formulating strategies to take advantage of them or change them. As Henry did, we can use the arrogance of our competitors against them, and as Don Burr did, we can address hidden motivations that customers might have.

But the most important mind to consider is that of the strategist. We need to recognize the pull of our desire for immediate gratification and accept that it isn't our conscious reasoning that directs our actions. Instead, it's our high-level beliefs and values that determine what we do. To ensure that we act in line with our long-term goals, we've got to keep in mind the vision of the future we're striving for and frequently check ourselves against it. But we also need to be willing to challenge the conventional wisdom so that we can completely reinvent the business the way CTP did. For in the world according to neuroscience, the mind of the strategist is a powerful competitive advantage, but only when it's disciplined and focused on the future.

SEVEN

CHANGING MINDS

The idea that someone would purposely try to drive a dolphin crazy is enough to stop us in our tracks. It seems so incomprehensible that we have a hard time making any sense out of it. We think of dolphins as those playful little mammals that always seem to have a smile on their faces and would never harm anybody. Why would anyone want to drive one crazy? How would anyone drive one crazy? What does it mean for a dolphin to go crazy? There don't seem to be any reasonable answers to these questions, and that's just the point. The same kind of frustration we experience pondering them is exactly what Gregory Bateson was trying to create in his experiment with driving a dolphin crazy.

Bateson was a man with incredibly wide-ranging interests. With his first wife, Margaret Mead, he had studied the indigenous culture of the Balinese and concluded that it was free of many of the conflicts that troubled ours. He went on to work with schizophrenics and formulated the double-bind theory, which proposed irresolvable dissonance as the cause of the disease. Later he participated in the design of the twelve-step process that Alcoholics Anonymous uses to help people overcome their battle against addiction. The theme that tied together all of his work was how people made sense of the world. He considered our Aristotelian logic to be plagued with problems, with schizophrenia and addiction as just two of the more extreme examples, and he saw a more natural use of the mind as preferable.

Since porpoises were believed by many to be more intelligent than human beings, they attracted Bateson's attention, and he spent the sixties and early seventies studying how their minds worked. Bateson felt that, like the Balinese, the way dolphins made sense of the world freed them from many of the problems that afflicted human beings in the developed world. But while identifying a better way of thinking is one thing, being able to adopt it is quite another. Ultimately he came to believe that the greatest challenge we face is change. His experiment with the dolphin was an attempt to understand under what conditions we would change from one way of thinking to another.

By this time, the theory of cognitive dissonance had established that our response to reward and punishment was not as straightforward as the behaviorists thought it was. The mind intervened: discounting, rationalizing, and ignoring dissonant information, driving behavior that didn't fit their model. Bateson wondered what would happen if the dissonance was of a kind that couldn't be so easily reduced by our Aristotelian logic. Would it cause us to change the way we think? His experiment was designed so that there was no way to make sense out of how a reward was dispensed, and so as a result, there was no way to respond logically.

He taught the porpoise a series of tricks and rewarded the performance of each trick with a fish, as expected. Next he stopped rewarding every trick and only gave a reward after three tricks were performed. The porpoise quickly became accustomed to this change. But then Bateson withheld the expected reward no matter how many tricks the porpoise did, and determined to only reward it when a completely new trick was performed. The porpoise responded by performing every trick it knew, either singly or three at a time. When it received no reward, it acted just the way George Homans had predicted: it got angrier and angrier.

But when there was still no reward after even more tricks, it started "to go crazy, exhibit signs of extreme frustration or pain. What happened next in this particular experiment was completely unexpected. . . . The animal not only invented a new trick (for which it was immediately rewarded); it proceeded to perform four absolutely new capers that had never before been observed in this particular species of animal." Caught in the dissonance between the expectation of reward and its absence, the porpoise, after much struggle, learned that new tricks were required for a reward.

We can think of it like this. The porpoise had learned to play the game of reward and punishment, and one of the rules was that "if you repeat the tricks, you get a reward." There was no rule in the game allowing for the invention of completely new tricks, nor was there a rule that allowed for changing the rules. In effect, the dolphin was imprisoned within the game. When Bateson didn't reward the tricks the dolphin already knew, he invalidated the rules and ended the game. No longer knowing what rules to abide by, the dolphin was initially frustrated, but then started generating random behaviors until it hit on the performance of a completely new trick. When it then received a reward, the dolphin realized it was playing a new game with the rule, "if you perform a new trick, you get a reward." It experienced a paradigm shift.

Bateson's experiment didn't just demonstrate how smart dolphins are. It captured a fundamental truth about what it takes for intelligent beings to change. We live according to an implicit set of rules that govern the way the world operates and specifies how we need to behave in response. We've called these rules Aristotelian logic. Given that we make our experience conform to the way we think the world is by reducing any cognitive dissonance, everything we encounter operates according to this set of rules.

The only way for us to change our thinking, and the behavior it gives rise to, is to realize, like the dolphin, that the rules no longer hold and the game has ended. For that to happen, we must experience "reversals of logic" that demonstrate the rules are no longer valid. The resulting cognitive dissonance can't be reduced by any other means than a new paradigm, which comes with a different set of rules.

Neuroscience teaches us that we can formulate more robust competitive strategies, design organizations that will perform at a higher level, and manage people so that they realize their fullest potential. All of these powerful insights come to naught, though, if we don't implement them, and that requires not just a change in behavior, but a change in the thinking that drives the behavior. Because the paradigm responsible for our thinking is self-reinforcing, the only way we can move beyond it is to experience the kind of dissonance that invalidates it.

Thankfully, neuroscience also teaches us how to create that kind of dissonance. It's through the skillful use of the counterintuitive. Our attempts to change the behavior of either individuals or organizations within the objective paradigm will fail because they will fall victim to relationship effects. But if we first use reversals of logic to invalidate the paradigm and change the way people think, we'll be able to get the kind of behavior we need to transform our businesses. Stories are the best way to create and manage this kind of dissonance.

WHY CHANGE FAILS

When the venture capital money arrived, one of the first things the founder did was plunk down $2 million to buy a ski chalet. As we stood on the porch, he explained that it would be a good place for the software developers to write their code. "They can sit out here and look at the mountains," he told me, pointing out the view. "It will stimulate their creativity." Although he had a well-earned reputation for being a bit over the top, I couldn't help but be impressed with this former professor's concern for the well-being of his people. The new ski chalet was the site of the strategic planning session we were holding with the executive team that afternoon.

We started the meeting after lunch. About an hour later, when the team was considering different strategic options, the founder jumped to his feet and proclaimed that the ideas being generated were worthless. "The only people in this room that aren't idiots," he announced, "are the engineers that graduated from Carnegie Mellon and Caltech." This excluded over half of the executives, most of whom were just business school graduates from Harvard and Wharton. The room grew silent, and there were looks of agony on the faces of the executives, regardless of the school they had attended. I decided it was an appropriate time for a break.

I took the founder aside and explained to him that his observation might very well be valid, and I could understand his disappointment, but the way he expressed it was detrimental to the team. It drove a wedge between the business and technical people, and the company's success depended on a strong cooperative relationship between them. I told him there were other ways to deal with his frustration, and I recommended that he briefly apologize when the meeting resumed. In my experience, it would head off any bad feelings that might derail our process, and, if anything, increase the team's respect for him.

When the meeting resumed and he rose to his feet, I expected him to make a brief statement that would get us back on track. "Let me be clear about what I said," he stated professorially. "The only people in this room that aren't idiots are the engineers from Carnegie Mellon and Caltech." With that, he promptly sat down. For all intents and purposes, the meeting was over. For the next six months, the company spun its wheels as most of the executives were either preoccupied with managing the founder or trying to avoid him. Finally, the venture capitalists bought him out and removed him from the company. By then it was too late. The window of opportunity for the company's offering had been missed, and $30 million in funding was gone with virtually nothing to show for it, except a ski chalet.

I don't believe that the founder was just blowing off steam or indulging a taste for making people feel miserable. I think he was genuinely trying to raise the quality of the ideas being generated. His attempt to improve how people were thinking was driven by the paradigm he used to organize his experience of the world. In the Newtonian universe, the application of a little force, in the form of punitive criticism, is what's needed to move people to change. Colloquially, it's known as a kick in the butt.

Of course, we know this would never work. Even leaving aside the fact that people generally don't have that kind of control over the quality of their intelligence, his approach came across as domineering, and like Achilles, human beings resent being controlled. His statement also created the same dynamic that hampered G.E.'s performance appraisal process, reinforcing the behavior it was intended to extinguish. It became in the best interests of those who weren't engineers to become even more idiotic, if possible. At the very least, he ensured that they would withhold their participation to avoid punishment, and there weren't many comments from the business executives, intelligent or otherwise, for the rest of the meeting.

Because I'm well aware of this dynamic, my attempt to change the founder's behavior was carefully managed so that it would not be construed as punitive. Instead of criticism, I acknowledged that the founder's comment very well may have been valid. Focusing on the goal we were all trying to achieve, I simply offered straightforward advice, although what might have been objectively reasonable to me wasn't necessarily so to him. Regardless, my reasoning didn't prove to be any more effective at creating change than his criticism.

Although Aristotle believed that people were rational and that superior reasoning would motivate them to change, we know it's not that simple. Emotion always plays a role in our decision making and we've all experienced it trumping our reason. Even though the founder saw his comments as perfectly rational, clearly there was emotion behind them and behind the way he responded to my advice. Even if he'd been coldly rational, he still would have reduced the dissonance created by my comments in favor of his position. That's what most of us do when our logic is being challenged.

The problem with both the criticism leveled by the founder and the neutral advice I offered is that both were attempts to drive change from the outside. While the application of force might work in the physical world—regardless of whether it's benign, punitive, or rewarding—it doesn't in the mental world. As Socrates demonstrated, people are more likely to change when the motivation comes from within, and when we ask rather than tell.

THE MORE THINGS CHANGE

The difficulty of changing an organization really came home to me when I worked for a telecommunications company trying to transition to a deregulated world. One of the managers hired me to teach his people how to participate in joint performance appraisals. His employees had nicknamed him "Thumper," because the data center he managed had a raised floor that sounded like a bass drum when he stomped across it. The training courses started at 8:30 in the morning, and if they weren't full, he would thump into people's offices and order them to attend, without the slightest concern for what they might be doing. The scuttlebutt around his group was that his management style had been honed when he worked as a POW interrogator during his time in the military.

A new performance appraisal system was just one component of a corporate initiative to change the culture of the company. There was also a new set of prescribed behaviors, along with a PR campaign and management seminars to promote them. These were targeted at creating a more participative work environment to foster the commitment and innovation needed to compete in the company's recently deregulated market.

One day, the committee that had been appointed to drive the initiative was to meet with its sponsor, a senior executive appointed by the CEO. On the wall of the conference room the meeting was held in, a poster trumpeted the initiative and listed the new behaviors. Within fifteen minutes, the executive had violated every one of them. None of the other people attending the meeting, all long-term employees, noticed anything out of the ordinary.

The CEO had undertaken this initiative because he was convinced that his new strategy would only be successful if the people responsible for its implementation radically changed their behavior. In fact, he was so committed to it that he saw the $25 million it cost as an absolutely essential investment. In this, he was far ahead of most of his peers. It's not unusual for a company to formulate a new strategy and then fail to execute it because the old organization remains intact. The CEO not only recognized the need to make the necessary structural changes, he was determined to address the critical issue of culture as well. The new behaviors listed on the poster were indeed the ones needed for the company to succeed. The problem was that no one other than the CEO really embraced them. The only thing the $25 million did was enrich a group of consultants.

In many ways, changing an organization is the sum total of changing all of the individuals in the organization. When a change initiative is based on the objective paradigm and designed with Aristotelian logic, reasons, threats, and/or incentives are the motivators for change. Because they don't work for individuals, we can hardly expect any different outcome with groups of individuals. But changing an organization is even more difficult than changing individuals, because direct contact, for the most part, is not an option. The change must be worked through the organization. Should there be a breakdown at any level, whether executive or managerial, the initiative will fail.

We're quite adept at reducing cognitive dissonance and maintaining a consistent view of the world, even when a conscious effort is made to change it. Thumper's employees didn't think for a moment that the training heralded a change in how they were going to be managed. They just assumed, in keeping with their view of his character, that the training was a corporate initiative he was being forced to go along with. Even the committee tasked with driving the initiative never believed that it was going to lead to real change. They'd been through so many other initiatives before that they referred to the current one as the "initiative du jour."

At a minimum, for a change initiative to take hold, all aspects of it must be aligned. The vision, the strategy, the organization, the culture, and the management practices need to be integrated. Even then, though, success is not guaranteed. The problem with Thumper and the executive was that while they might have bought the need for the initiative and knew they had to support it, they never really believed in it. It's just not possible for all behavior to be hardwired, and because behavior is ultimately driven by what goes on in our minds, the nuances of our behavior will communicate what we really think. A change initiative is only going to work when the way we think changes.

Even if all aspects of the organization were aligned to support the initiative and it addressed the way people think, its chance of success would still be questionable. Because our minds are automatically reducing cognitive dissonance, we don't necessarily become aware of information that is at variance with our view of the world. The only way we'll be prepared to accept the possibility of change is when there's a marker we're forced to attend to that proclaims the world is going to be different going forward. Otherwise, odds are nobody will even notice that there is an initiative in place.

And there's still one other issue that makes change so difficult. While our Aristotelian logic leads us to believe that we're separate from the world, we are enmeshed in a network of interdependent relationships. Because what we do affects others and what they do affects us, actions don't always produce the results we expect them to, as we saw with price-cutting strategies in the automobile industry. The cognitive paradigm captures these relationships, and the effects we get when we attempt any kind of change are not unlike what happened when we first used the insecticide DDT. Not only did the insects die, but so did the birds that ate the insects, the predators that ate the birds, and so on through the food chain until the DDT started to poison us. There were unintended consequences.

Systems scientist Jamshid Gharajedaghi believes that "the actions intended to produce a desired outcome may, in fact, generate opposite results." As an example, he points to the war on drugs. The U.S. government has spent billions of dollars to fight drug use, but the result has been the unintended consequence of creating a huge criminal enterprise to supply drugs. The harder it is to bring the drugs into the country, the higher their cost, the greater the profitability, and the more attractive is the business to criminal elements. This powerful industry now thrives on the fact that the drugs are illegal, and of course, does everything it can to create and supply demand.

Relationship effects are, as we've seen, at work in the use of reward and punishment. Increasing the motivator of extrinsic reward can decrease intrinsic motivation, and punishment can end up reinforcing the behavior we're trying to extinguish. Because the relationship effects are obscured by our Aristotelian logic, we may not even recognize that our actions have a result that is the opposite of what we intend. Instead, like Porter Goss at the CIA, perhaps we'll simply blame the culture.

THE ILLOGIC OF CHANGE

A farmer is particularly proud of his mule and boasts about its wonderful qualities frequently. One day he's talking to his neighbor and going on and on about how terrific this mule is. It's smart as a whip, he claims, works tirelessly, and will do whatever you ask it to. This last claim is finally too much for the neighbor.

"How can you brag that your mule will do whatever you ask?" he demands. "Mules are stubborn, and I've never met one even half as obedient as you claim yours is."

The farmer is unfazed by this challenge, and responds that his claim is indeed the truth. But the neighbor is unwilling to accept what he's sure is an exaggeration, and demands, "Show me!"

So they go out to the barn, and there in the back is the mule in a stall. They walk toward the stall, and just as they get there, the farmer bends down, picks up a two-by-four, and smacks the mule over the head with it. Caught by surprise, the neighbor asks, "What are you doing? You said your mule was obedient and would do whatever you asked."

The farmer replied, "Yes, he will, but you've got to get his attention first."

Getting his attention first is exactly what Bateson had to do in order to get the dolphin to change from repeating old tricks to creating new ones. We are very much prisoners of our paradigms, attending to information that confirms them and cleverly reducing any that is dissonant. The only way to escape from the paradigm is to stop its automatic processing. Two-by-fours may work with mules, but a little more subtlety is necessary for human beings.

At a biological level, our paradigms are neural circuits that have become acclimated to a set of inputs, perceptions, or ideas. When the expected input occurs, there is a minimal level of neural firing in response. But if the input is different than expected, a host of new neurons fire. The two cerebral hemispheres appear to be quite specialized in this regard. Neuropsychologist Elkhonon Goldberg believes that "the right hemisphere is particularly adept at processing novel information and the left hemisphere is particularly adept at processing routinized, familiar information." What captures our attention and stops our automatic processing, according to neuroscience, is the new.

This startling revelation is, of course, not so startling. As journalists say, "Dog bites man is not news; man bites dog is news." If the conscious mind were an evolutionary adaptation to enable us to respond flexibly to the unexpected, as many cognitive scientists believe, it makes perfect sense that the new would grab our attention. In the absence of the new, our mental processes proceed automatically and unconsciously. One way of thinking about the new is that it is anything contrary to our expectations. It stops us and forces us to stand back and reflect.

Studies have shown that it does take longer for us to process novelty than the expected. We know from *f*MRIs that the unfamiliar creates heightened activity in the prefrontal cortex. Biologically, the unexpected is responsible for more firing in the area of the cortex thought to be the site of reflective consciousness, and in the right hemisphere of the brain that processes wholes. Psychologically, it pulls us back and directs our attention to the big picture. We become aware that something is amiss with the game we're playing—the paradigm we're using can't make sense out of what we've experienced. We're ready to entertain new ones.

But it's not just anything unexpected that will have the effect we want when we set out to change the way people think. It's got to be the kind of dissonance that can't be reduced by any of the other strategies we like to employ, such as ignoring, discounting, or rationalizing. Because the rules of the game we're playing are Aristotelian logic, we need reversals of logic, the counterintuitive, to get the result we want.

Social psychologists have found that dissonance of this kind stops our brain's automatic processing and forces us to question the validity of the paradigm we use to structure our experience. Rather than keeping our view intact by reducing the dissonance, we change the way we think, revising or scrapping our model of how the world works and the appropriate way to behave. Rather than change the input to the model, we change the model.

We undergo a "cognitive restructuring" to create a "new integration." Our existing worldview is swapped for one that incorporates the dissonance and resolves what had appeared as a conflict. This happens when the dissonance is at such a high level that it is "embedded in a large network of knowledge, beliefs, and feelings," when it's valued and embraced rather than feared and avoided, and when there is no other viable way to reduce it.

Perhaps the most common experience of this kind of dissonance is failure. When we are successful, there is no reason to reflect on what we're doing or change it. Success positively reinforces our current way of operating. But when we fail, our automatic processing is stopped. We are then driven to ask questions, to dig deeper, and perhaps to change how we think and behave. It is thought that the big step forward in how the early Greek scientists made sense of the world was their active search for information that would disconfirm their theories, in contrast to the ancient Egyptian tradition of blindly accepting received knowledge.

This is why we euphemistically refer to failures as "learning experiences." Rather than shunning them, they should be embraced and mined for any insights into how we can operate better. While our tendency may be to protect our fragile self-image, it is far more productive for us to challenge it. Instead of looking for instances of confirmation of our views, we should actively seek out disconfirmation. When someone offers to give us feedback, we really should think, "Oh great, I'm going to have an opportunity to improve."

USING THE COUNTERINTUITIVE TO DRIVE CHANGE

Not only does the counterintuitive grab our attention and serve as a marker of change, the actions that make change happen will also frequently strike us as counterintuitive. For example, rather than continue to fight against drug use, a growing number of law enforcement professionals believe we should legalize it. Such a step would eliminate both the expense of fighting drugs (including housing abusers at great expense in prisons) and profits for the criminals. Without those profits, criminals would leave the industry, and the supply would decline. The money spent on enforcement could be reallocated to treatment and programs encouraging people to abstain. The fear, of course, is that the level of abuse would rise when drugs became legally available. The opposite, however, has been the case in European countries where use of safe, nonaddictive drugs, like marijuana, is not aggressively suppressed. The experience of Prohibition also supports legalization.

Similarly, a counterintuitive action is the best way to change the dynamic of an escalating conflict. In a disagreement in which both parties raise their voices louder and louder until they're shouting at one another, lowering one's voice not only has a calming effect, it eliminates any reason for the other party to yell. Its illogic subverts the logic of the other person, breaking the vicious cycle of feeling compelled to respond to the action of another with more of the same.

Psychotherapist Paul Watzlawick explained why the counterintuitive works so well by drawing a distinction between ". . . two different types of change: one that occurs within a given system which itself remains unchanged, and one whose occurrence changes the system itself." Actions within a system he called first-order changes, and they will appear eminently reasonable in a world that operates according to Newton's laws of motion. Force needs to be matched with force, violence with violence. These are the kind of changes that create the relationship effects we've seen at work in price-cutting strategies and the use of reward and punishment. It was first-order change that I used in my attempt to persuade the founder to apologize.

Watzlawick calls actions to change a system second-order changes, and they will appear to those within the system as exactly the opposite of what should be done. These are the counterintuitive actions like competing in Prisoners' Dilemma to get cooperation, legalizing drugs to cut down on their use, and attacking the French when logic says you should be in a defensive position. As Mahatma Gandhi showed, responding to violence with nonviolence ends the vicious cycle by invalidating the logic of escalation. The rules no longer hold, and the game is changed.

Watzlawick illustrates the difference between first- and second-order change with the example of a couple on a sailboat. To balance the boat, the man sits on one side and the woman sits on the other. The man moves a little further out, unbalancing the boat, and the woman is forced to move out to rebalance it. As she moves out, the man moves out to counter her movement and regain the balance. This competitive dance continues until both are hanging way off their respective sides of the boat. In other words, they are in a relationship in which their behavior is interdependent. Each move out forces a counterbalancing move out on the part of the other. This is first-order change.

Their sailing trip could be a lot more comfortable if they were sitting further in, more securely inside the boat. The solution is for one of them to do exactly the opposite of what they have been doing to maintain the balance, and paradoxically it will initially destroy the balance rather than improve it. One of them just has to move in, forcing the other to move in as well. Inside the boat, this would be counterintuitive. From outside the boat, where one can see the big picture, it is clearly the only solution. This is second-order change.

Watzlawick demonstrates the power of second-order change in his treatment of a young couple burdened with overly attentive parents. When the parents come to visit, the mother cleans, and the father does all the household repairs, regardless of the couple's protestations. The parents also insist on paying for groceries, restaurant bills, and any other expenses that come up during their visit. The couple is frustrated by this overdose of parenting and would like it to end. They have already tried the logical solution. They vigorously cleaned the house and made any needed repairs before the parents' visit. During the visit, they fought to pick up restaurant checks and to cover the cost of groceries.

Demonstrating that they did not need their parents' help was to no avail. Apparently, the parents envisioned the game as one of positive escalation. They must have thought that the more they did for the couple, the more the couple did for themselves. There was no reason to change their behavior because it obviously was working. The house was clean and in good repair, and the couple was working to keep it that way. So Watzlawick's advice to the couple was to do exactly the opposite. Rather than demonstrate their independence, they needed to demonstrate their dependence.

Following his advice, they made sure that the house was particularly dirty and in need of repairs the next time the parents came to visit, and they eagerly let the parents pay for any and all expenses. As a result, the parents decided to cut their visit short, explaining to the couple that they were becoming too dependent on the parents for help. When the couple was striving for independence and the house was well taken care of, the parents had, in their view, been good parents by helping the children, and so their behavior was reinforced. But when they saw the couple becoming more dependent on them, they recognized that their behavior was not producing the results they wanted, and good parenting had to be redefined as letting the "overly dependent" children fend for themselves.

The way to come up with the appropriate counterintuitive action, according to Watzlawick, is to change the "conceptual and/or emotional setting or viewpoint." Changing the paradigm we use to make sense of a situation will highlight the action we need to take. In the physical world of Newton's laws, force needs to be matched with force. In the mental world of interdependent relationships, we should take the action we believe will cause the other person to behave the way we want them to. An easy way to change the conceptual setting is to set aside our point of view, and use our theory of mind to adopt the other person's point of view. When we do, we'll realize that the action required for change is usually the opposite of what we think it should be.

We've already seen how powerful the counterintuitive can be in strategy. At the battle of Agincourt, their unexpected attack transformed the weakness of the English into a strength. We've also seen how the less control we exert as managers, the more we get the behavior we need, and the less structure in our organizations, the better the performance. We've even seen that sometimes the best way to sell consulting services is to tell the prospective client that they don't want them. All of these actions fly in the face of our Aristotelian logic but make perfect sense in a mental world that operates through natural selection.

Unfortunately, we can't accept as a rule of thumb that we just do the opposite of what our reason would suggest. It's risky to tell someone aiming a gun at us to shoot, and responding to a competitor's price cut by raising ours isn't necessarily a viable strategy. But if we swap out the objective paradigm for the cognitive one, we'll get a view of the situation that will account for relationship effects. We can then determine what action to take to get the kind of response we want.

In the mental world, we don't find the direct connection between cause and effect that we do in the physical world, as the use of reward and punishment illustrates. So the best approach is to determine under what conditions the target of our change effort would behave the way we want, then take the counterintuitive action needed to create those conditions. In other words, determine what the rules of the game need to be and then do what it takes to invalidate the current game and establish a new one with the rules we want.

If we want people to start focusing on the work and not the reward, we can take a salary of only a dollar to dramatize our commitment to the company, as Lee Iacocca did when he took over as the head of a bankrupt Chrysler. If we want to break down the hierarchy and create more participative management, we can move our office from the fiftieth floor of our headquarters to the second, as John Reed did when named CEO of Citicorp. If we want to create a more informal, team-based approach to getting work done, we can show up at the office on our first casual Friday without our toupee, as one authoritarian manager at Bethlehem Steel did.

Because such actions are counterintuitive, they stop the automatic processing and signal that change has occurred, and because they're aimed at changing the way people think rather than eliciting a direct response, they avoid those self-defeating relationship effects. However, there is still a need for all actions to be consistent and send a unified message. The best way to ensure that is through a vehicle perfectly suited to change the way people think, the story.

CHANGING STORIES

As we've seen, using stories to change behavior is more effective than logical declarations. Because they don't proclaim truth, they don't create relationship effects or elicit attempts to refute them. They're the way our minds naturally work, so they're very accessible. Addressing both our intellect and our emotion, and the two hemispheres of the brain they reside in, they have a more profound effect than an argument. By calling our attention to relationships and environment, they prevent us from falling victim to the effects of first-order change. But the most powerful aspect of stories is their ability to fundamentally change how people think by pivoting on dissonance, a core attribute first noted by none other than Aristotle.

If we think back to stories we've experienced, our tendency is to view them as explanations. Starting with the state of affairs at the end, we recognize the series of events that caused it. The fall of Troy was caused by the abduction of Helen. The death of Hamlet was caused by his rash response to the murder of his father. The failure of People Express was caused by Don Burr's immature orbital frontal cortex. But that's not the way we experience stories in real time. We don't start at the end and look back. We start at the beginning and move forward.

When we experience stories in real time, they're about planning: having a goal with a sequence of actions to accomplish it. But a story about a plan would not hold much interest for us. It's when the plan doesn't work, when the implementation fails because something contrary to expectations occurs, that a story has its greatest value for us. Psychologist Jerome Bruner believes that "the impetus to narrative is expectation gone awry. . . ." Stories are, first and foremost, a way to deal with dissonance.

The overall plan of our strategist, Odysseus, is to sail home to Ithaca, but the action of the epic revolves around the series of obstacles he encounters. Aristotle called an obstacle of this kind a *peripeteia* and defined it as a change "from one state of things . . . to its opposite." Just as when the porpoise didn't receive the reward it expected for a trick it performed, the peripeteia alerts us to the fact that the world is not as we thought. So just like the porpoise, when we are immersed in the story, we search for a way to deal with it. As Bruner puts it, "The story concerns efforts to cope or come to terms with the breach and its consequences. And finally there is an outcome, some sort of resolution."

But unlike the porpoise, we experience the dissonance within the context of the story. We don't have to suffer a series of trials and errors. The resolution is given to us. Rather than it occurring randomly, the process of change can be managed. Like a counterintuitive action being selected so that it causes the game we want to be installed, the peripeteia can be selected to ensure the kind of resolution that is desired.

When we think of change this way, it becomes much easier to come up with those counterintuitive actions that Watzlawick believes are critical to second-order change. The beginning of the story is a given, for it's the current state. The end of the story is the future we desire. We have a clearly defined strategy for our organization and everything is in place for its implementation. The dissonant event, the peripeteia, is what it takes to stop the way people are thinking now and create the new way of thinking that will drive the behavior we need to achieve the future state.

It would be difficult to imagine a more boring story than one about a company that increases its return to shareholders or one about a firm on the verge of bankruptcy that cuts its expenses and returns to profitability. But all too often, this is the story that management tells. A story that's going to engage people needs to be a romance in which people accomplish great, meaningful feats. For Bethlehem Steel, the story was about people working together as a team, overcoming a history of arrogance and mistakes to save a great American icon. For Cambridge Technology Partners, the story was about David slaying the Goliath of the IT business with a slingshot of superior intelligence.

The test of the peripeteia is whether it gets us from the present to the future in a believable way. When we watch the movie in our mind's eye, we have to be convinced that it works and we can buy it. It's believable that a steel company under threat of bankruptcy would abandon the perks of management, particularly when it installs self-managed teams and moves to a new building, complete with a new sign and an opening ceremony. But it's less believable that an automobile company with a history of ineffective change initiatives, a lineup of uninspired cars, and an intact hierarchy is really going to change this time around.

That's the other great benefit of a story. It forces us to attend to every detail if it's to be believable. The setting, the characters, and the action all must be aligned. Nothing can be out of place, and there can be no mixed messages. An effective initiative that's going to change how people think is like theatre. Every scene must be perfectly crafted, every role precisely performed, and all of the action flawlessly executed.

DISSONANCE THAT CAN'T BE REDUCED

The discoveries of neuroscience make it clear that there is a much better way to think about business, a way that leads to more powerful strategies smoothly implemented through smart organizational designs and effective management. But these new ways of doing business only have value if they're put into practice, and that requires change. Unfortunately, the approaches to change our Aristotelian logic drives are doomed to fail. In the mental world we inhabit, cause and effect are not as directly linked as they are in the physical world. Reward and punishment all too often produce the opposite of what we intend, and reason is notoriously unconvincing to those that don't already agree with its conclusions.

The problem is that our minds have evolved to maintain the

status quo. As a species, we are quite good at reducing any dissonance that threatens our view of the world, including the kind that
might motivate us to change. But paradoxically, it's this same ability to reduce dissonance that makes it possible for us to change.
When the dissonance is at a high level, when it's counterintuitive,
and when it's of the kind that can't be easily reduced any other way,
it can drive a paradigm shift that will change both how we think and
how we behave.

This kind of dissonance renders the logical rules of the game
invalid. We are then prompted to recognize that there is a different game with different rules. When change is well managed, the
new game drives precisely the kind of thinking and behaving that
our change initiative targets. While, in certain cases, just doing
the opposite of what's expected will create the dissonance we need,
more often than not, it's better if we start with the kind of thinking
we want and create the dissonance that will lead to it.

Working through a story is the easiest way to do this. Stories
pivot on the peripeteia that changes how we think, and as we've
seen, stories affect us in very profound ways. To create a story to
manage organizational change, we specify where we are and where
we need to be, and we look for the kind of event or marker that is
both believable and will lead us from the one to the other. But to
really be effective, the story should address our higher aspirations
and be presented with the same passion and attention to detail as
great theatre. It is the role of the leader to make sure that happens.

EIGHT

LEADING IDEAS

One of the more curious findings of neuroscience is that I don't exist. I do have a social security number, a place of work, and a home address, so in the eyes of the government, my professional colleagues, and my family, there is indeed a Charles Jacobs. But my sense of who "I" am, the identity I've honed for a lifetime and that occupies me from morning to night, is only an illusion. This isn't just my issue—your "I" is an illusion as well.

But as sure as I'm sitting here, I know that I exist. I can look down and see myself as I type on my laptop, my arms reaching out and my hands over the keyboard. I can distinctly remember getting up this morning, going for a run, and eating my breakfast. When I turn to look at the table next to my chair, I can see a picture of myself with my family when we were on vacation last year. If I needed any more evidence, I'm quite aware that I'm thinking about all of this, and according to René Descartes's dictum *Cogito ergo sum*, that's proof enough that I exist.

The problem is that all of this evidence runs smack up against the results of a simple experiment that would seem to prove that I don't exist. When two images are flashed on a screen in succession a short distance apart, it appears that a single image is moving from the location of the first to the location of the second. This psychological effect is known as the phi phenomenon, and we're quite familiar with it because it's how movies work. Although a film is just a succession of still images, we infer movement from seeing one after another and experience the action as seamless.

If we introduce color into a demonstration of the phi phenomenon, though, something very odd happens. When a red dot is lit for a fraction of a second and then, after a brief interval, a green dot just a short distance away is also lit for a fraction of a second, the red dot appears to move toward the location of the green dot, just as in the black and white version. But then about midway, its color miraculously changes from red to green.

We know that the dot isn't really changing color, that it's just an illusion created by the subsequent lighting of the green dot. But we see the dot change color *before* the green dot is lit. This is impossible unless we can foretell the future and know that the green dot will be lit. Even if this were the case, how would we explain what happened to the original red dot when we saw it turning green?

The results of this experiment fly in the face of common sense. We know we can't foretell the future, so how do we explain the dot changing color? The answer offered by neuroscience is to accept that there is no "I" that exists over time. There's no connection between our perception of the red dot and our perception of the green dot, because the "I" that thinks there is and perceives the change in color is just a figment of our imagination.

Our common sense holds that there is an "I" that perceives the world around us and controls our thoughts and actions. It is often envisioned as a little man or woman who resides in our head, a homunculus who sits back observing and controlling our life. When our attention is directed elsewhere, it is the homunculus who does the directing. Most of us also feel as if there is a homunculus existing in the heads of those we interact with.

But, of course, there's no homunculus in our heads or anyone else's. Our skulls are chock-full of brain cells, and there's no room for a little person. Setting aside this folk image, there's also no part of the brain that corresponds to a screening room or control center. Even if we accepted the idea of an "I" that directs our attention and controls our actions, despite the phi phenomenon, we'd still be faced with the question of who or what directs it.

According to neuroscience, our perceptions of the world exist as the firing of nerve cells in local networks distributed throughout various areas of the brain. We become conscious of any given one when our attention is drawn to it and it becomes part of a larger network linking more areas of the brain. There can be a number of such perceptions existing simultaneously, and Daniel Dennett suggests that we think of these as "multiple drafts," different ways of making sense of our experience.

Depending on whatever else is going on in our minds at the time, one draft or another will be favored because it's a better fit. Although each is as discrete as the individual frame of a movie, our experience of them over time yields "something rather like a narrative stream or sequence." In the case of the phi phenomenon, the draft of the moving red dot is replaced by the draft of the moving green dot, and we see the dot appear to change color. In the case of "I," the succession of drafts creates the illusion of an identity existing through time in the same way that the succession of still images creates a movie.

The implications of the multiple-drafts theory cause many people to violently object to it. If there is no "I" existing over time, there need be no reason to assume personal responsibility for one's actions. A clever lawyer could mount a defense claiming that the defendant standing in front of the court is a person different from the one who committed the crime. We'd have to accept that the spouse sitting across from us at dinner is not the same person as the one we married. In fact, the one who ate the entrée is different from the one eating dessert. Even more disconcerting is the fact that the "you" who read the previous page is a different "you" than is reading this one. While common sense tells us that this is ridiculous, we must remember that common sense is, according to neuroscience, also just one of the multiple drafts created by the firing of a distributed neural network.

It doesn't cost us much to hold on to the illusion that there is an "I" and to continue to believe that the spouse we greet at night is the same one we said good-bye to in the morning. But we can no longer trust that either our view or theirs is an objective record of what happens or that we have the ability to control our thoughts or events in the world the way we thought we did. A world that is created anew every moment requires very different ways of thinking and behaving than the stable and enduring one we thought we inhabited.

The phi phenomenon raises a fundamental question about leadership: if there is no "I," just who or what does the leading? The answer neuroscience gives us challenges our conventional view of a leader as one that is in charge. Rather than view leaders as dominant alphas, it makes more sense to see them operating like Socrates. In place of forcefulness, they need an understanding of the minds of those they set out to lead and the aspirations those minds create. As in the case of management, organization, and strategy, historical models help us create a profile of what it takes to be an effective leader in business. But we also have the benefit of good hard data about which leadership practices produce the best results.

LEADING BILLIARD BALLS

At the beginning of the movie *Patton,* the biopic of the famous World War II general, George C. Scott walks out on a stage with a gigantic American flag as a backdrop to address his troops. He's dressed impeccably in a uniform of his own design, with jodhpurs tucked into riding boots, a waistcoat covered with medals and accented with a blue sash, a steel combat helmet, and an ivory-handled pistol. Planting himself firmly, he begins his speech with that raspy trademark voice at a volume that makes it clear he's in command.

He starts out by telling his men "no bastard ever won a war by dying for his country," but by making "the other poor dumb bastard die for his." Patton was a student of history with a belief in his own reincarnation, and he had learned the lessons of Odysseus well. With these inspirational words setting the tone, he goes on to clarify his expectations. "I don't want to receive any messages from the front that we are holding our position," he orders. "We're not going to hold on to anything. . . . We're going to advance constantly and go through the enemy like crap through a goose." Patton had also learned the value of a well-turned metaphor.

He follows up this image with another one of cutting out "the enemy's guts and using them to grease the treads of our tanks." To address any concerns the men might have about their courage, he tells them that they'll know what to do when they stick their hand in "a pile of goo" that used to be their best friend's face. Such frightening and graphic images suggest that in Patton's leadership model, fear is a powerful motivator.

When we think of leaders, we often get an image like the one Scott conveys of Patton. The courage and raw power he projects are similar to what made Achilles such an attractive hero to the Greeks. We view him as strong, dominating, and courageous, without any second thoughts or hesitation. We can see him charging headlong into battle at the front of his troops, but we certainly can't imagine him disguised as a beggar and allowing insults to be heaped on him by his wife's suitors, like Odysseus.

There is research substantiating that this kind of authoritarian leadership does work when there is a crisis and people are accustomed to being given direct orders. Besides, Patton had demonstrated success in battle, and all soldiers would prefer a glorious victory over defeat and death. But everything we've learned about the mind and relationship effects would lead us to predict that Patton's approach would ultimately backfire, and it did. All of Patton's great accomplishments in battle were quickly forgotten when he attempted to motivate a shell-shocked soldier to return to battle by slapping him repeatedly in the face. Shortly after, the general died in disgrace.

Patton's model of leadership has had an enormous effect on the business world. For most of the last half of the twentieth century, the men, and they were mostly men, running our large corporations had learned about leadership in the military during the Second World War. Orders, the use of force, and intimidation became their preferred tools, and their necessity was justified by the aggression and passivity created by their use. When times change, the organizations and cultures that shape our behavior don't necessarily change at the same rate. The objective paradigm and the leadership it gives rise to are still firmly entrenched.

We've seen Patton's style of leadership in the founder of the software company haranguing his managers, in the president of the steel company seeing participative management as a waste of time and money, and in Thumper barging into people's offices. It's become legend in Donald Trump's "you're fired" and in the antics of the "Queen of Mean," Leona Helmsley.

I've run into it repeatedly throughout my career in ways that border on the comic. I've witnessed the CEO of a health-care company demand at an executive meeting that the COO fix the leak in his private toilet because he was in charge of operations. I watched the president of a household goods manufacturer throw his glasses at his vice president of manufacturing and, when asked why he did it, answer that he had nothing heavier to throw. When my first consulting firm was acquired, my new boss told me I acted like I had a burr under my saddle, as if I were a pack animal, and asked the CEO in my presence what he could "force" me to do.

Although there is something that we can't help but find attractive about Patton and wish to emulate, when it comes right down to it, his leadership is simply not effective. While fear and veiled threats will get compliance in the short term, we know that they stimulate aggression. We do find strong leaders comforting, particularly in times of crisis, but the relationship effect produces lower self-confidence and difficulty deciding what to do when there's no one shouting orders. Besides, slaps in the face have never motivated anyone to do anything other than slap back.

The deeper problem is that Patton's leadership model doesn't fit the world of thinking beings. In the physical world, there is an agent for every action. Somebody has to use the cue to impart force to the billiard ball. But as the phi phenomenon demonstrates, that's not the way the mind works. Our thoughts and behavior aren't controlled by us or by anybody else. They are driven by the narrative draft that fits best with the mental environment. Leadership isn't about forcing people to do our bidding, but about telling a story so that they want to do what we need.

WHAT LEADERS NEED TO KNOW

Weighing in at close to five pounds, with twelve hundred pages of double-columned small print, and subtitled, *Theory, Research &*

Managerial Applications, Bernard Bass and Ralph Stogdill's *Handbook of Leadership* is not the kind of book one reads just to pass the time. In fact, it's not the kind of book that many would read at all. It's a compilation of thousands of studies on leadership, presented one after another after another. Few in the business world bother with it, and that's a shame, for this book is a treasure.

There aren't any hot new models, five-step processes guaranteed to produce dramatic improvements, or anecdotes extolling companies that were successful because they did A, B, and C. But there are well-documented descriptions of carefully controlled studies of every conceivable approach to leadership, along with the results each produces. It's full of just the kind of hard data managers love, and all of it is directed at making them more successful.

While the experience of reading it is just what you would expect from its appearance, every so often you come across a finding that just stops you dead in your tracks. There's the study that reviewed pay-for-performance programs, which are a fixture of most corporations, and found no linkage between pay and performance. There's another one that found reward and punishment are actually effective, as long as the work is "repetitive, boring, and tedious." Then there's the one showing that the effect of a reward depends not on what it is, but on the employee's perception of the manager's reasons for giving it.

There are also a wealth of studies on authoritarian and democratic leadership, directive and participative decision making, and the results of focusing attention on people versus production. We learn which kind of leadership works best with intellectually challenging jobs and with mindless ones, with skilled employees and unskilled ones, and with managers who have knowledge of the work and ones who don't. We find that some forms of leadership improve employee satisfaction, others increase performance, and still others improve teamwork. There are even studies on what kind of leadership works better for the long term or for the short term.

The problem with the handbook is that there is so much information in such detail that readers don't walk away with any better understanding of what kind of leadership they should embrace. There are just too many interdependent variables to consider and too many different kinds of leadership to choose from. Stogdill himself claimed that there were as many different definitions of leadership as there were people defining it.

Determining what works best in a given situation is even more difficult because leaders aren't very good at recognizing what kind of approach they're using. According to a study of 360-degree feedback programs referenced in the handbook, what leaders think they're doing is not the same as what their employees think. Managers are consistently rated lower on key dimensions of leadership by their employees than they rate themselves, especially when it comes to being participative.

But there's one message that comes through loud and clear in the book, and it's that transactional leaders are less effective than those who hold out the promise of transformation. *Transactional* leadership, as the name suggests, is a simple exchange. Most commonly, it's work from the employee for money from the leader, but it can include other kinds of exchanges, such as loyalty for job security, friendship for consideration, and commitment for opportunities to develop. This kind of leadership is what defines most managerial relationships.

Transformational leadership is very different. It is not about an equitable exchange, but about the opportunity for employees to become fundamentally changed if they sign on to follow the leader. What changes, of course, is the way the follower views the world and thinks and acts as a result. This kind of leadership is often seen as charismatic or inspirational, and it offers the prospect of employees realizing a more profound purpose in their work. The relationship with a transformational leader is more exciting, and followers are more engaged.

It was the political scientist James McGregor Burns who first used the terms "transactional" and "transformational." In his 1978 classic, *Leadership*, he offered the likes of Winston Churchill and Franklin Roosevelt as examples of transformational leaders. Both men came to power during a time of crisis and enabled their followers to triumph over adversity so severe that they'd never seen the like before. While both called on people to make great sacrifices, they held out an attractive vision of the future that would be realized as a result. People were asked to change, and when they did, they achieved more than they thought possible.

While we might like to think of ourselves as a Churchill, most of us in the business world are transactional leaders, and the odds are that we're managing an exchange with our people based implicitly on the use of reward and punishment. Because most managers are uncomfortable with punishment, they shy away from it, leaving them with only rewards at their disposal. Other than the limitations we've already noted, the problem with rewards is that they can only reinforce current behavior. There is no way for a transactional leader to drive the kind of fundamental change we refer to as transformation.

Given the limitations of reward and punishment and the way big ideas work on the mind, it should come as no surprise that transformational leaders consistently outperform transactional ones. This is true whether we're looking for a quantum leap or just incremental improvement, for transformational leadership has been demonstrated to increase performance even when just used to supplement transactional leadership. We may not be facing anything comparable to the Battle of Britain, but we should still aspire to be transformational leaders simply because it's more profitable. Besides, it's a much greater challenge for the leader and a lot more fun for the followers.

A PORTRAIT OF A TRANSFORMATIONAL LEADER

It's the beginning of what is shaping up to be the greatest challenge you and your people are likely to ever face. You've bet your career, and right now the odds aren't looking all that great. Even though everybody knows that you're way overmatched, you've tried to put the best face on it you possibly can. Then just at the moment when you need all the support you can get, your top guy starts to grumble about needing more resources. It's the last thing you need to hear, and certainly you can be excused for giving free rein to your anger.

But that is not how Henry V chose to respond at the battle of Agincourt, at least according to Shakespeare. When Westmoreland, his cousin and one of the captains of the English troops, wished for more troops from England, Henry's response was to give what has come to be seen as perhaps the greatest transformational leadership speech ever, inspiring the likes of Winston Churchill and John F. Kennedy. Even though Shakespeare's version is "just a story," it is perfectly in line with what the research tells us a leader needs to do to be effective. It's just a bit more accessible than wading through Bass and Stogdill's abstracts, and as stories do, it addresses the feelings as well as the intellect.

While most of us would probably be tempted to answer Westmoreland with a sharp rebuke, the young king didn't see his captain's remark as a problem, but as an opportunity to assuage the doubts probably all of his men shared. Henry sees the small number of troops as an opportunity and not a problem. He tells his captain and his troops that they don't want any more men. If they have more and lose, there will just be more men who die. If they have more men and win, they'll just have to share the glory.

Four centuries before scientific research had established the key dimensions of transformational leadership, Shakespeare gives us a perfect example in the character of Henry V. Methodically, the king goes on to address every issue needed to inspire his troops. Though he is the supreme commander, he refuses to order his men into battle against their will, and offers them money and transport if they decide not to fight. Of course, there's nothing wrong with stacking the deck in favor of the decision he wants with a statement like, "We would not die in that man's company / That fears his fellowship to die with us."

Now that Henry has their attention, he gives them not one, but two visions of the future they're fighting for. "From this day to the ending of the world / But we in it shall be remembered," he tells his men, holding out the promise of immortality. This is certainly inspirational and raises the stakes to a grand level, but most of us would prefer a payoff that we don't have to die to get. So he paints a picture, with just enough detail, of a holiday they'll celebrate in the future, sharing a mug of ale with their friends and showing off the scars from the wounds they received at Agincourt. Without antiseptics, the greatest fear next to death would be a wound, for it would almost certainly prove fatal. But just as he did with the number of troops, Henry shifts how his men think about the prospect of being wounded.

But Henry's not done yet. Given the potential for relationship effects, Henry cannot be on a pedestal. In the most frequently quoted lines of the speech, he demolishes the hierarchy: "We few, we happy few, we band of brothers. / For he today that sheds his blood with me / Shall be my brother." But enticing as the promise of brotherhood is, Henry must bring his men back to focus on the present moment if he is to get the best performance from them possible.

So he returns to those men home in England whom Westmoreland had wished for. They are not the fortunate ones, Henry proclaims, for they "Shall think themselves accursed they were not here." We're back where we started, but with a critical difference. We have experienced Aristotle's peripeteia, and the battle and the men's place in it are now seen as the opposite of what they were before. The world is transformed and the men are transformed.

What a contrast with Patton's speech before his men went into battle! There's no demand to constantly advance, emphasized with a graphic image. Instead, it's up to Henry's men whether they'll fight or not. In place of "a pile of goo," a wound is likened to a badge of honor. Nor are there any "dumb bastards." The men are brothers to one another and to their king. While Henry holds out the promise of transformation, all Patton offers to inspire his men is the statement that "all real Americans like the sting of battle."

Henry's greater effectiveness comes from his ability to empathize with his men, create a romantic counternarrative, and present it in a way compelling enough to transform their view of the world. At the same time, he is as humble as Socrates, preferring the place of a brother to his spot on the pedestal, and like Socrates, Shakespeare's Henry knew the world he inhabited was mental. His final words to his troops as they go off to battle are, "All things are ready, if our minds be so."

Of course, it's neither fair nor scientific to use fictional portrayals to argue for the superiority of one leadership approach over another. But Henry's speech does illustrate everything we've noted effective managers do, and what Bass and Stogdill tell us transformational leaders do. Leaders who inspire outperform any other kind, not just on the battlefield, but in business as well. Besides, stories are just paradigms, and Henry's gives us an apt model for business leadership.

TRANSFORMATIONAL LEADERSHIP IN BUSINESS

It's doubtful that any of us in business will find ourselves facing death and the defeat of our country like Henry. Most of us would also look ridiculous in a doublet and tights, spouting Shakespearean verse, and promising immortality to our followers. But given the limitations of transactional leadership and the proven capacity of transformational leaders to improve both the performance of the business and the satisfaction of the employees, it makes sense for us to figure out how to carry over to the business world what Henry does in this speech. We can boil it down to five key actions.

SHIFT THE PARADIGM. Given the mind's ability to reduce cognitive dissonance and configure our experience of the world so that it agrees with our beliefs, expressing anger won't work to change people, nor will reason. What will work is to transform how people think about the world, particularly when times are tough and a turnaround is needed. A failing business can be seen as an opportunity to break with the past and redesign the business the way you want it to be. Or you may want to present turning around the business as the challenge of a lifetime, one that if your people can pull off, will give them the confidence to do just about anything. If there just doesn't seem to be any way to put a better face on things, you can simply acknowledge the situation and stress the fact that there is no option but to deal with it the best way they can.

MAKE IT PARTICIPATIVE. Bass and Stogdill present numerous studies demonstrating that participation improves both performance and employee satisfaction. There are caveats on the use of participation, as when employees are new to their jobs and lack the skills and knowledge to make informed decisions. But studies of 360-degree feedback show that our employees rate us as less participative than we rate ourselves, so odds are we won't be participative enough. We can probably err in the direction of too much participation without much risk.

CONVEY AN ASPIRATIONAL VISION OF THE FUTURE. As we saw in Henry's speech, the vision of the future should take people beyond themselves, but it should also have a more immediate experiential appeal. In business, all too often, the vision is neither aspirational nor experiential enough. When the CEO of a telecom company announced to his four hundred top managers that his vision of the future was "an increase in shareholder value," his audience, not owning nearly as many shares as he did, responded with a collective yawn. One manager later facetiously remarked to me that if the CEO had been alive, he never would have given such a speech.

The vision also needs to be credible, not too much of a stretch. No one is going to buy that a fast-food restaurant is going to make the world a better place, but employees will buy into a vision of having the most satisfied customers of any outlet in the industry. The prospect of creating a new product, service, or new way of doing business can be very inspirational. "Changing the way the world thinks" worked for the employees of Digital, while the potential to save jobs and pensions was more than enough for people at Bethlehem. For most of us, it's just doing what we do as well as we can and striving to be the best, whether we're designing a chip, making steel, or serving fast food to hungry customers.

Just as we saw with stories, the more experiential the vision is, the more powerful it will be, so the achievement of the vision should be made as tangible as possible. This can be done by creating a picture of what it will be like when the vision is realized. Maybe it's the scene in the office the day your customer satisfaction ratings are the top in the industry, or maybe it's the setting of the celebratory dinner when you sign that new customer.

TELL THE STORY. As we've seen, people are going to embrace a story to make sense of their experience. As the phi phenomenon suggests, there is no "I" that creates this story. Instead, our attention is drawn to any one of the stories that exist in our neural network, based on its fit and how appealing it is. A transformational leader offers a counternarrative that is a more attractive version of events than the story people are currently telling themselves. Perhaps Westmoreland's story was about the defeat of the English army while the desperately needed troops lounged at home in bed. Henry's counternarrative was about a band of brothers performing heroic feats.

All too often, the story employees tell is about just getting by, about incompetent and venal management, or about destructive corporate politics that make it not even worth trying. The counternarrative is easy to come up with. People join together, change the way they work, and accomplish great deeds. As Henry's speech demonstrates, this story can be told with a few key details that evoke scenes, like the scars and the mug of ale. Its power is in the fact that it addresses more than just the intellect and is not a logical argument that has to withstand scrutiny. It would be easy to demolish Henry's case for having fewer men.

We shouldn't underestimate the power of the story. Given that we create the world, rather than record it, and that ideas in high-level neural networks create thoughts and behavior in line with them, even one idea can cause far-reaching changes in the way the mind works and transform both us and the world. During the last half century, social psychologists have repeatedly proven the power of ideas to change minds and behavior.

One experiment demonstrated an effect similar to that of Henry's explanation of why more men weren't desirable. A college class was informed that they would have a guest lecturer. Half of the students were given a description of the lecturer that included adjectives like "cold," "industrious," and "critical." The other half's description was exactly the same, except the adjective "cold" was replaced with "warm." After the lecture, the students rated the professor. Those who were told he was warm gave him significantly higher ratings than those who were told he was cold. During the class itself, the "warm" group participated more and asked more questions. The differing evaluations were based on the same observable behavior.

The students were primed with an idea, just as a leader's story primes the minds of the followers, but the effect isn't limited to how people perceive a situation. In a psychological effect known as the self-fulfilling prophecy, an idea really does objectively alter the world. A change in perception affects behavior in a way that causes the new perception to become true.

Researchers administered an IQ test to students at an elementary school. Afterward, their teachers were told that some of the students were "bloomers," and would show significant IQ growth in the coming year. In reality, the students were average, but when tested again at the end of the year, they showed a marked increase in IQ scores. The teachers behaved differently toward the "bloomers," and that caused them to develop in line with the teachers' expectations.

These experiments teach us how to control the creation of another's reality. If we prime our family with the belief that dinner is going to be wonderful, on average they will tend to experience it that way. If we tell the cook that he or she is wonderful, he or she just might perform at a higher level. If we really believe that someone is wonderful, we might unconsciously do things that will make the person wonderful. In one landmark study in the business world, priming was used to dramatically increase the performance of salespeople. With just one idea, we can not only change how people think and act, we can improve the quality of their thoughts and actions. The most powerful way to convey that idea is through a story.

CREATE FOCUS AND URGENCY. Henry had no need to create any more urgency or to focus his troops. The presence of the vastly larger French army did it for him. In a corporation, though, it's easy for people to become complacent, so it's important for the leader to let the followers feel the competitive pressure, but not to the extent that it makes them insecure. The leader also must make sure that people stay focused on what's critical for success. If the key to winning is customer satisfaction, selling, or expense control, it should be a critical part of the leader's story, and it should be repeated often enough to cause structural changes in the neural networks that drive the necessary thinking and behaving.

THE CHARACTER OF THE LEADER

The distinction between transactional and transformational leaders was translated into terms more familiar to the business world by Abraham Zaleznik in a seminal article in the *Harvard Business Review* entitled "Managers and Leaders: Are They Different?"

He saw managers as the direct heirs of Frederick Taylor, primarily interested in incremental improvements. In contrast, he saw leaders as creative, concerned with ideas, and viewing themselves as agents of change. From his perspective, much of their power comes from having been through a traumatic experience and emerging from it stronger than they were before. Since they are effectively "twice born," they are highly empathetic and able to help others work through the discomfort of change.

There might just be something to this notion of a twice-born leader. None of us would question the strength, courage, or effectiveness of John F. Kennedy, Winston Churchill, or Franklin Roosevelt. We look back at these three as strong, charismatic men, but there were questions about the character of all three earlier in their lives. Churchill had a penchant for self-promotion even when it required a bit of fabrication, Roosevelt was a wealthy playboy, and Kennedy's main asset seemed to be a father willing to buy elections when necessary. But each encountered failure or trauma, and as Zaleznik suggested, drew strength from it.

The character and heroics that Churchill displayed during the Second World War were preceded by the eight years he spent on the sidelines after his leadership was rejected by the British people. Roosevelt's transformation of the American economy and psyche during the Great Depression followed his devastating bout with polio. Kennedy's brilliant leadership during the Cuban missile crisis came after the dismal failure of the invasion of the Bay of Pigs that ended with the United States abandoning the invading Cuban troops. All three of these men were first humbled by personal failure, and only then demonstrated the empathy that made them so successful as leaders.

Henry, too, had encountered hard times in his life, and he was well aware of his own fallibility. This enabled him to accept people

for who they were and not think he could force them to be something else. The kind of character needed to be a transformational
leader seems to start with an acceptance of one's own fallibility. By
the same token, the software company founder's punishing criticism of others is right in line with his inability to acknowledge his
own mistakes. If we're Don Burr, we don't even think for a minute
that our pursuit of an expensive, unionized airline could be a mistake, nor do we admit it even after it bankrupts our company.

Which brings us back to the phi phenomenon. We can see how
easy it is to get people to embrace a counternarrative as their own
when instead of an "I" creating stories, the mental environment
selects out one of the many available. All the leader needs to do is
to offer a story that is more attractive. But if there's no "I," what or
who is it who creates the story and offers it? The clue to the solution
of this puzzle is in how we experience failure, and it's the reason
twice-born leaders are so effective.

When we experience dissonance, as the dolphin did, it stops
our automatic processing and creates activity both in the prefrontal
cortex and in the area of the right hemisphere of the brain responsible for the perception of wholes. Failure on a grand scale, which
our leaders experienced, is just the kind of dissonance to cause
this to happen. Effectively, our attention is drawn to the existence
of more than one paradigm, or draft, as Dennett would call it. The
self-monitoring of the prefrontal cortex would then learn that one
paradigm could be a better fit than another.

The new mental environment, shaped by the failure, would
select out the paradigm that was a better fit, and this paradigm in
the form of a story would guide the thinking and behavior of the
leader. The story communicated to the followers would be the same
one the leader was telling himself. Without a story firmly in place,
we'd be just like Don Burr, at the mercy of our nucleus accumbens.

In order for leaders to consistently think and act in line with the story they tell, they've got to really embed those neural networks by believing the story and telling it over and over. Perhaps the best way to think about character is that it's an unswerving belief in the story we tell.

Transformational leadership is about rewiring our minds and those of others by telling a more fitting story, so the only tool the leader has to effect change is communication. But we can't just hurl graphic metaphors in a loud voice and trust the Newtonian laws of motion to get the result we want. We need to focus on the *relationship* with the receiver, and we need to recognize that the relationship is a function of the *environment*. Patton's "crap through a goose," experientially moving as it is, probably wouldn't play very well in today's business world.

While our three twice-born leaders had styles very different from Patton's, they were all equally effective at communicating their story. Churchill's power was in his bulldog expression, bow tie, and steady voice intoning phrases like "the world may move forward into broad, sunlit uplands." For Roosevelt, it was the pince-nez glasses, the cigarette holder, and the calming voice telling us "there is nothing to fear but fear itself." Kennedy's youth, good looks, and tousled hair were all part of the package that convinced America to "ask not what your country can do for you, but what you can do for your country."

Each of these men had a unique style of leadership that was very much a function of his character and the situation he found himself in. What works during war won't necessarily work when there's peace, what is effective in one country might fail in another, and what succeeds in the political environment probably won't play well in a corporation. I've seen a painfully shy, soft-spoken PhD effectively energize his R & D group with a halting, almost inarticulate speech. It wasn't nearly as entertaining as Patton's but it fit the followers and the environment. I've also witnessed a high school dropout with a vocabulary limited to four-letter words and a mouth full of chewing tobacco fire up steelworkers. What both had in common is that their style of communication fit who they were and the needs of their followers. They believed the story they were telling, and so they were authentic.

While what one has to do to be a transformational leader is pretty straightforward, the need to communicate expressively can be a bit intimidating. However, there is consolation in what we've learned about how the mind works. Through both priming and the self-fulfilling prophecy, people become what we think they are, as we saw in the case of the guest lecturer and the children who were identified as bloomers. While we're not big fans of bosses, we do like leaders. In fact, we hold the expectation that our leaders will be charismatic. If they can just avoid doing anything offensive, that expectation will become a reality.

STORYTELLING

The findings of neuroscience have eliminated many of the tasks associated with the traditional approach to management. Given the failure of reward and punishment and other extrinsic ways of motivating behavior, managers have no choice but to consistently put the responsibility for performance back on their people. At the same time, there is an even greater need for the kind of leadership that changes how people think. In a mental world, it is ideas that shape behavior, and it is the transformational leader's job to package the right kind of ideas into a story and to effectively communicate it to the organization.

Essentially, the only thing leaders have at their disposal is communication, but the example of Henry V shows that it's really all they need. He doesn't shoot the messenger who voices doubts all of the others share but instead takes his concerns as an opportunity to understand the mind-set of the followers and change the way they think. He makes sure that it is the men's decision to fight, and he articulates a vision of the future to motivate them. Teamwork is stressed, and to guard against creating dependency, he steps down from his pedestal. When we apply this model to the business world, it becomes a template for what a transformational leader needs to do in a corporate environment.

While a George Patton comes across with the strength and courage we usually associate with leadership, we know from neuroscience that it won't have the effect we want. The kind of leadership that works is more humble and therefore more empathetic. We see it in the likes of Churchill, Roosevelt, and Kennedy. Perhaps because they knew what it meant to be human and fallible, these leaders, with very different styles, communicated ideas that took people beyond themselves to accomplish more than they ever thought possible. That's the kind of transformation organizations need and people long for.

NINE

ALL THINGS ARE READY

Tracing the flow of information through the brain with an ƒMRI leads to the rather surprising conclusion that we can't possibly have the direct knowledge of the physical world we think we do. All we can know is its representation in the brain as ideas, so the world we experience is mental, not physical. The chair you're sitting in, the book you're holding in your hands, and even your own body, are just creations of your mind. This is not an easy notion to get our heads around, but it is a scientific fact with far-reaching ramifications for how we think and act.

Rather than sharing the same world, we all inhabit a world that is uniquely our own. Our backgrounds, experience, genetic make up, culture, thoughts, and feelings all affect how we put together our versions of reality, and it's a good bet there will be wide variations among them. Men and women, adults and children, managers and employees, customers and suppliers, liberals and conservatives, Christians and Muslims, all will see the world differently. So will identical twins.

At some level, we accept this difference. We acknowledge that people see certain clothing styles as more attractive than others, believe some foods taste better than others, and evaluate some potential mates more favorably. We recognize a wide range of views about everything from the nature of God to whose sports team performs the best. But we tend to believe that these differences are relatively minor shadings and that we all have the same core experience. So we are surprised when our different versions of reality collide. We're amazed that other people thought O. J. Simpson was innocent (or guilty if we believed him to be innocent), that our spouses really thought our behavior was self-centered, and that our managers believed 5 percent was a suitable salary increase, given all that we'd achieved during the year.

Even though the world of ideas we inhabit operates differently than the world of physical objects, our minds trick us into thinking and acting as if it doesn't. So we tend to see other people as if they're physical objects like stones or trees, and we don't pay enough attention to how they make sense of the world. Believing they, too, are governed by Newton's laws of motion, it seems we can move them around like pieces of furniture. But because people don't like to be forced to do anything, our actions don't produce the results we expect. In fact, they often produce the opposite of what we expect.

Although our view of the world entails a unique way of thinking as well, our minds take the way we think as the only way there is. We assume the laws of logic govern how we think, and there's no provision for how our thinking might distort what we think about. But our minds don't work through syllogisms. Our ideas are arranged in hierarchical networks, and any idea can affect other ideas by changing the chemistry of the brain. Rather than obeying the laws of logic, our reasoning is a competition of ideas, with the best one selected out by the mental environment. Our decisions, no matter what we think to the contrary, are made as much by our emotions as our logic.

If this isn't enough to get our heads spinning, there's the person who supposedly directs all of this. On that matter too, we appear to be operating under an illusion. There is no part of the brain that corresponds to an "I," and the mind doesn't function as if there is one. Much of our reasoning takes place without our conscious knowledge of it, there is no central clearinghouse for our perceptions, and we lack a consistent identity. We can't even trust the fidelity of our perceptions, for the memories that enable us to recognize them change each time they're accessed.

It's as if we live in a world that is a figment of the imagination, but we can't even claim that it's *our* imagination. This world has no physical basis that we can know and no continuity from one moment to the next. It doesn't operate according to the laws we think it does, nor do we think the way we believe we do. Alice's Wonderland seems sane by comparison, but at least she knew something was a little wacky. We refuse to believe that the world is anything other than what we've always believed it to be. It's just the way the mind works.

AND THE GOOD NEWS IS . . .

Even if the "I" is just an illusion, it's a serviceable one. We live our lives, keep body and soul together, strive for deep meaning and purpose, and have moments of great joy. In fact, most of us have lived our entire lives under the illusion of an "I" and an objective, orderly world, and have never noticed anything amiss. That's one of the charms of our minds. They're quite good at reducing any uncomfortable dissonance between the way we believe things to be and the way they "really" are.

Besides, neuroscience doesn't just leave us adrift in this strange world. It offers us a way of thinking and a way of acting that are a better fit with the real nature of the world and so are more effective. It teaches us that our view of the world is biased and that we need to account for how it differs from everyone else's. It enables us to avoid those self-defeating practices that haunt us with their unintended consequences, and to make use of the relationship effects that create them. Like a self-help book, it promises the keys to greater success and more happiness, but with the added benefit of actually being based on scientific research.

Although our views of the world are subjective, our minds also come with a remarkable ability to empathize, which enables us to appreciate the versions of reality that others live. We are able to step into the shoes of people, and see the world as they do. Paired with our instinct for storytelling, empathy lets us identify with their story and anticipate how they will behave. We can then figure out how we need to act to get the response we want. It may not be as direct and immediate as the use of the carrot, stick, or logical argument, but it has the advantage of producing the results we intend.

The world we can know doesn't operate predictably according to Newton's three laws of motion, but Darwin's concept of natural selection does a pretty good job of capturing how it does work. Although it doesn't give me the certainty of predicting where a billiard ball will come to rest, I can anticipate what will be the results of the way I act in a relationship, and I can use that information to my benefit. I can't move ideas around the same way I thought I could, but I can shape the environment to select out the ideas I want. It may not be as simple as what I'm used to, but it works.

My Aristotelian logic may not be how the mind works or a suitable way to think about the world of human activities, but a Platonic dialectic is. I can play one idea off another to come up with a better, more comprehensive idea, and that idea will then select out other ideas and behaviors in harmony with it. Rather than force my argument on people who will simply turn it to their advantage, I can shape their thinking with ideas and use questions to guide them to reach the right conclusions on their own. It may take longer, but they'll be more committed to the result.

At first, the new tools neuroscience gives us may seem a little daunting to use. It does take more forethought and more time to formulate and implement a strategy to encourage someone to willingly do what we want. A billiard ball world is easier to understand and manipulate than one that is a network of interdependent relationships. But these tools work better because they fit the nature of the world we live in. Our ability to reduce cognitive dissonance may obscure the failure of actions driven by our common sense, but they still fail.

MANAGEMENT ACCORDING TO NEUROSCIENCE

Because we're not managing in a physical world but in a mental world, much of what is taken for granted as the right way to manage is actually the opposite of what we want to do. But to be more effective requires only a simple shift in perspective. Instead of seeing the world through the lens of Newtonian mechanics, we start seeing it as a process of natural selection. Rather than viewing people as inanimate objects, we recognize that they're thinking beings acting of their own volition. Because of the way the brain is organized, if we can just keep this perspective in mind, we'll know the right things to do.

In the Newtonian world, all action is through the application of force. In the world governed by natural selection, any action elicits a countervailing action, just as one person leaning out on a sailboat requires the other person to lean out as well. Because of these relationship effects, direct actions don't create the results we want, so we're better off making use of the forces that are already at play. The management revolution is about no longer *forcing* people to do things but *encouraging* them. Because behavior is driven by thinking, management according to neuroscience is about changing minds.

Competition is force against force in the Newtonian world, with the strongest coming out on top. In the mental world, the key to competitive strategy is to leverage how the other side is already behaving or influence them to behave the way we want them to. We use our power of empathy to understand how they will respond to different actions, then select the one that gets the response we want. We may need to prime people to see things differently or make use of relationship effects.

When it comes to business strategy, competitive advantage is established by creating an offering the customer wants and the competition can't duplicate. This requires understanding how the customers think, so you can make your offering appealing to them, and understanding how the competition thinks, so you can configure your offering in a way they aren't disposed to match. Sometimes the best place to start is with how you think. Taking a counterintuitive view can highlight ways of differentiating a product or service others would never think of.

The same basic principle is at work when implementing the strategy. Rather than forcing employees to do something, we want them to do it willingly. For managers, this turns the world upside down. They don't tell, they ask. They don't dispense rewards, punishment, or feedback that can be construed as either. Instead, they work for the employees, acknowledging the selfish gene, and making use of their energy, desire for accomplishment, and need for compensation. They put the responsibility for performance on the employees and supply the information and support that enable employees to self-manage.

When it comes to organizing large numbers of people, we'll get better results if, rather than trying to thwart their natural inclinations, we just accept how people behave and make the most of it. People do want to become part of a group when it's kept small, when the advantages of collective effort are stressed, and when the competitive threat is clear. We can structure organizations as federations of small entrepreneurial businesses, the relationships between them managed through free-market dynamics. Profit is substituted for salary, and selfishness is aligned with the goal of collective effort.

But the ultimate solution may be to leverage minds. Human beings will always come together in support of causes they believe in, and such collective effort doesn't require cumbersome structures and control systems. Besides, no matter how much structure is in place, it is never enough to prescribe all behavior. The rest is covered by what we have come to call culture. As the collective story the group tells itself, culture drives the thinking that drives behavior.

Strategies that leverage the mind and don't use force, management that works for the employee and doesn't try to control the uncontrollable, and organizations that operate just the way natural selection does—all will lead to better performance with less stress. But all require change, and that has always been the sticking point for efforts aimed at improving business performance. While the mind is quite adept at reducing the dissonance that argues for change, even convincing us that we've changed when we haven't, it is through creating dissonance that we are able to transform people and organizations.

But it's got to be the right kind of dissonance. Bateson's dolphin changed the way it thought when it didn't receive the expected reward and realized the game had changed. Because the game humans play is structured by logic, the illogical is the kind of dissonance needed to change the way we think. Taking a salary of a dollar a year or refusing to wear the toupee you've worn every day for twenty years is the kind of counterintuitive marker needed to alert people that the world is no longer the same.

Stories can effect change without the frustration the dolphin was forced to suffer, because they offer a ready-made way to resolve the dissonance. It's the role of the transformational leader to create the story that identifies the kind of change needed and to present it in a way that is meaningful and moving. It should align the needs of the individual with those of the organization, so that people see the necessary changes as a way to meet their desire to be part of something bigger than themselves and realize their fullest potential. At the same time, it must be immediately appealing. Immortality might be attractive, but most of us would prefer a payoff that doesn't require our demise.

The story needs to be communicated powerfully in both words and deeds, and it needs to be as experiential as possible for people to relate to it. This requires some skill, and the best leaders are emotionally expressive. Even so, their style should fit who they are. The strongest are often the ones who come across as the most humble, for, given the potential for relationship effects, leaders must step down from their pedestals so that followers don't become overly dependent.

There is plenty of data that links this management approach to superior performance, and there's no lack of anecdotal evidence showing that today's cutting-edge companies are managed this way as well. As we've seen, it's all supported by the latest scientific research on how the mind works. But even beyond this validation and the simple fact that it creates a better environment for people to work in, this kind of management is aligned with our deepest values. It brings democracy to the workplace.

From its invention in ancient Greece to its American incarnation two millennia later, democracy has consistently created superior performance in all domains of human activity. The Golden Age of Greece followed right on the heels of the establishment of democracy and witnessed accomplishments in the sciences and arts never since equaled. Although under a bit of stress lately, the American democracy is the world's leading economic and cultural power. Is it democracy that's responsible? In a survey of civilization's greatest economic powers, economist David Landes answers affirmatively. The open-mindedness fostered by democracy creates the entrepreneurship that drives superior economic performance.

But there's always been another case made for democracy, a moral one. It is simply the right thing to do if you believe that all people are created equal. Because of this, an approach to management aligned with the latest discoveries of neuroscience speaks to something profound in all of us. It addresses both our need for individual freedom and our desire to join together with other people to accomplish more than we ever could by ourselves.

THERE'S MORE TO LIFE

It's not just business that benefits from the insights of neuroscience. We use the same mind to make sense of all of our experience and to determine the best way of acting. When we shift paradigms and factor in how the mind works, our reading of the different situations we find ourselves in becomes more accurate, and the actions we take as a result are more effective. We get better at dealing with the most intellectually demanding dimension of our lives—our relationships with other people.

In all aspects of our lives, we should take advantage of the evolutionary adaptation that gave us the ability to think strategically about our relationships. Although it may be a rather jaded way of looking at the world, it's best if we take the notion of the selfish gene to heart and assume that all people are out for themselves. We can then figure out what they want by calling upon the ability to empathize that our mirror neurons and theory of mind enable. The more information we take in about them, the better we'll be at imagining the story they're telling themselves.

Once we know what they're after, we can then formulate a strategy that presents doing what we want as a way for them to accomplish what they want. In most cases, the strategy we need to employ will be straightforward. As Socrates taught us, it's better to ask than tell, but as Henry showed us, we can phrase the question in a way that will get the response we want. We may also want to prime the mind up front. If we're trying to encourage an airline gate agent to get us a seat on a crowded flight, expressing our dissatisfaction with our treatment by the airline and demanding what we believe we deserve is probably not going to get us very far. But commiserating with the harried agents and asking for their help, while expressing admiration for the job they do under such pressure, just might.

But there are times when a bit more is called for, usually when you're trapped in a competitive dynamic and are the victim of relationship effects. When a police officer pulls you over for a traffic violation and comes across as a bit belligerent, arguing that you weren't speeding isn't going to get you very far because it just feeds the competition. Instead, showing the officer the deference he or she would like may turn the dynamic to your advantage, just as it did when I agreed with the bankers that I wasn't the one to do the job.

We should also accept that no one ever wins an argument.

Inevitably, reason is countered with reason, and emotion with emotion. The facts are irrelevant, because each side will just use them to construct their argument. Counterintuitively, though, if one side stops arguing and acknowledges that the other side's point of view is valid, it defuses the situation and reduces the level of emotion. Just like one person moving in on a sailboat, it encourages the other side to do the same. It then becomes more possible for each to hear what the other one is saying and perhaps find common ground.

Strategizing relationships makes perfect sense, but it's easier said than done. The demand for his priestess kicked Achilles' amygdala into high gear, and it made no difference to him that his behavior then became self-destructive. The only hope we have of avoiding a similar fate is to self-prime our minds. When Odysseus is tempted to kill his wife's maids, he steadies his mind by talking to himself, so that it selects out patience rather than violence. The key to success, as we learned from the sea snail, is repetition. If I entertain an idea enough, it will reinforce the neural network by causing more synapses to grow and lowering the threshold needed for firing.

In the same way, the more I think about the importance of strategizing relationships and the more I practice it, the more it will become a habit of mind. Just the act of reading this book has rewired your brain and established new neural networks. Continuing to think about the ideas that are in it will develop habits of mind that will make you more effective in both work and life. But as neuroscientists put it, you must "use it or lose it."

NOW

So what do you do now that you've finished this book? Even though the ideas have been seeded in your brain and are shaping the mental environment at this very moment, the business world is action-oriented. Somehow, just contemplating big ideas doesn't seem like enough. Ever since Frederick Taylor, there's much to be done and not enough time to do it in. So it's going to require a lot of fortitude and discipline, because you need to take time out to stop and think.

Our emotions may make better gambling decisions in card games, but they can also lead us to kill our bosses and jeopardize the causes we've been fighting for. We do inhabit a mental world, but our reasoning is a product of our experience in the physical world, and it doesn't take into account those counterintuitive relationship effects that come back and bite us. So it's best if we slow down a bit, think strategically about the situation we find ourselves in, and then decide what action to take.

Think about opting for indirect rather than direct action. It's so quick and so easy to tell people what to do or to tell them how badly they're doing it. It takes longer to come up with questions to help *them* decide what to do or realize that their performance isn't cutting it, but the questions produce a better result. Questions build commitment and overcome the resistance to being controlled. They enable us to gather information that we may have assumed we already knew. And because people would rather talk than listen, questions build goodwill.

Questions are also a great way to change a disadvantageous competitive dynamic. The next time someone is arguing strenuously for his or her point of view, rather than arguing back, try asking a question, and see how the emotional level drops. Then listen to the answer and repeat it back in your own words. All of a sudden, the other person no longer has to fight so hard for airtime, or stubbornly hang on to one position. The relationship effect may have your opponent asking *you* questions in return and actually hearing what you have to say.

Another thing to stop and think about is consciously using nat-ural selection as a lens through which to view your experience. All of a sudden, you'll see things differently. You'll start to realize how much of what you do is a function of your relationships with others and how much of what they do is a function of their relationships with you. You'll see how much control you actually do have over other people, even though it may be indirect, and why an unreason-able action may be just what the situation requires.

Using natural selection as a lens will also alert you to how much we're a product of the environment and direct your atten-tion to ways of shaping it to your advantage. It will then become easier to abandon force in favor of creating the conditions that will encourage people to do what you want them to do. Next time you're in a difficult relationship with someone at work, try taking that person out for lunch or a drink, and see how it changes the interaction.

Rather than vainly fighting against the way things are, some-times it's best to just let it play out. If you interrupt people when they're talking, instead of listening to what you have to say, they'll just be waiting for an opportunity to interrupt you. But if you let them talk, eventually they'll run out of steam and be more willing to hear what you have to say. As I learned at the bank, the best sales calls are usually the ones in which the prospect does most of the talking.

You might also want to think about consciously making more use of stories, both to understand and to shape how people think and act. When we tap into the stories others are telling themselves, we gain a clearer understanding of who they are and why they do what they do. We become better able to predict how they will respond, so that we can generate the kind of actions that will get the response we want. Understanding our own story gives us a better sense of who we are and why we act the way we do, perhaps allowing us to avoid actions that are self-defeating. Stories are the most useful tool we have in the mental world. They have a unique power to sneak up on people and change the way they think and behave.

Even though it makes us uncomfortable, we should think about actively seeking out dissonance. Our minds are geared to quickly reduce it before we even become conscious of it, but it is dissonance that teaches us and changes the way we think. That critical feedback we dread stops us and makes us reflect. A position that conflicts with ours broadens our thinking and leads us to bigger ideas. From pondering the phi phenomenon to seeing our theory of human behavior fail, the dissonant is what broadens us and makes us grow. We shouldn't shun it or rationalize it away. We should seek it out and savor it.

Perhaps the most important thing to think about is that the world is of our own making. In the world of Newton and Aristotle, we're subject to the slings and arrows of outrageous fortune, and our defense is to counter them with force. It's easy for us to see ourselves as victims of that forbidding and hostile world out there. But according to neuroscience, we are the creators of the world, and we can change it just by changing our thinking. We may no longer have the comfort of seeing ourselves as victims, but we can make the world anything we want it to be.

Paradoxically, one last thing we should think about is to spend less time thinking. Consciousness gave Odysseus the ability to stop and think rather than simply responding emotionally the way Achilles did. It is this ability that allows us to delay immediate gratification for the promise of greater gratification in the future. Rather than spending their days lounging around and eating what was at hand, our ancestors decided to till a field, plant seeds, and tend crops, for the bigger payoff of a harvest in the future. As both Odysseus' success and a trip to the supermarket show, acquiring conscious-ness wasn't such a bad deal.

But once this pattern of thinking is established, it becomes a habit of mind. It's applied to everything, and all of our behavior becomes goal-oriented. We focus on the reward we'll achieve, the promotion we'll get, and the career we'll enjoy. But this runs counter to the way the mind works. The nucleus accumbens releases its dop-amine when we're engaged in the work that leads to the accomplish-ment of our goals, not when we accomplish the goals. It's the work itself that is rewarding. If we're always anticipating the payoff in the future, we never get to enjoy the present moment, nor apparently do we bring our full capability to what we do.

Psychologist Mihály Csikszentmihályi found that when people were able to exclusively focus on the work at hand, they felt happy, self-fulfilled, and performed at peak levels. He called this *flow:* "the state in which people are so involved in an activity that nothing else seemed to matter . . . people will do it even at great cost, for the sheer sake of doing it." The pleasure, Csikszentmihályi believes, results "because a person must concentrate attention on the task at hand and momentarily forget everything else." Consciousness is focused and dopamine is flowing freely.

It's ironic, but the strategic brain that makes us so good at man-aging human acitivity prevents us from performing at peak levels and experiencing the pleasure that comes from total immersion in our work. As in so many aspects of the world according to neurosci-ence, the solution is to subtly shift our attention. When we need to be strategic about human affairs, we pull our minds back to the big picture. But when we're involved in our work, we zero in on the task at hand with a laserlike focus.

A century and a half ago, the novelist George Eliot wrestled with this same dilemma in the story she told of a young man who asks if he will ever become good at his work. His boss answers yes, but explains that "you must love your work, and not be always looking over the edge of it waiting for your play to begin." For all of its great discoveries and insights, neuroscience has no better advice to offer us than this simple little story.

APPENDIX: REWIRING THE BUSINESS

It's a wonder that groups are capable of any purposeful behavior at all, given that we're all operating off competing versions of reality and genetically hardwired to look out for our own interests. Even though we've evolved a social brain to facilitate our relationships with others, the tension between our selfishness and our altruism causes organizations to be inherently inefficient.

Performance would improve substantially by doing nothing more than getting everyone on the same page and cooperating. But if we could also harness the combined brain power of the organization to create a plan for moving forward, the gains would be much greater.

How can managers make this happen? It's as simple as getting people together in a room to decide what needs to be done and how best to do it. Not only does this build a shared understanding, it produces the most comprehensive view of the business and the best ideas. It also ensures the buy-in that is critical for implementation and energizes the team to make changes that may have been resisted before.

But groups can easily become unruly mobs and the operations of our brain are anything but perfect. The emotions of the moment can hijack the thinking of a group just as they do an individual, and the selective perceptions of individuals can add up to no more than groupthink. The chances of success are much greater if the group has a structured process to work through, and the recent findings of brain science suggest one.

AN EVENT TO REMEMBER

Our minds just continue their automatic processing until something grabs our attention, and the collective mind of an organization is no different. For a business to change, there must be a convincing marker signaling that the organization is serious about life being different going forward. Holding a meeting for people to rethink the business is just such a marker, and it keys a positive emotional response. People become engaged and experience greater control over their destiny.

The event should not be portrayed as simply another operational review, nor should its avowed purpose be to cut expenses X percent. Nobody gets excited about either of those prospects. Instead, it should be framed as an opportunity for people to participate in creating a new future for both the business and themselves. The business will achieve its goals, which in turn will enable the people to achieve theirs.

But creating excitement is just the first step. Rewiring the business requires changing the way people think and the way they behave. Once we have everyone's attention, it must be directed at creating a clear picture of what will be different in the future and laying out specifically what people must do to achieve that future. The outcome of the session should be a plan with well-defined action items.

Nor should rewiring the business be a long, drawn out process. There is little tolerance for meetings that always seem to go on for too long, and the rest of the world is not at a standstill. The environment is constantly changing, customer needs are evolving, and the competition is working as hard at finding an edge as you are. The desire for thoroughness must be balanced against the need for speed.

So the group members need to limit the scope of their work, restricting themselves to a high level plan and broadly outlining what needs to be done and who's going to do it. This should then be handed off to those responsible for its implementation wherever possible, both to encourage participation and to leverage the knowledge of those closest to the work.

It's also necessary for the group members to work with the information they have at hand—in my experience, they usually have more than enough. In areas where there are shortfalls, subject matter experts can be invited to participate. If the group decides further analysis is important, it can be undertaken after the meeting is over, and any necessary amendments can then be made to the plan.

Three days is optimal for such an event. It's enough time for the critical work to be done, it allows for the kind of immersion that pulls people away from their everyday concerns, and it's just short enough not to dampen enthusiasm for the result. Whenever possible, the meeting should be held offsite to minimize interruptions and to provide some distance from the immediate demands of the business.

THE TOOLS

The process of rewiring the business works best if before diving into the business, team members address how they interact with one another and how they make decisions. They can be prompted to stand back and reflect on how they work together, either by participating in a decision-making exercise unrelated to the business or by just brainstorming a list of what they like and dislike about their meetings. They can then formulate a set of behavioral guidelines to improve, such as "encourage all team members to participate," "listen to one another," and "withhold judgment."

Creating the guidelines heightens awareness of what behavior works best, and if they're written up on a flipchart and posted on the wall, they can be used as a subtle control system. Team members can call on the guidelines to address any behavior that hampers their effectiveness. Rather than provide direct critical feedback to individuals, with all of its limitations, participants can simply address the group with a question like "Are we listening to each other?"

The team will also work better with a structured decision-making process. When based on what we've learned from brain science, it will leverage the way the mind works and account for both the environment and relationships. Ideas are generated through brainstorming and, where possible, played off one another. They are then evaluated against an agreed upon set of criteria, with the one that best meets the demands of the environment selected out.

For example, a discussion of competitive strategy might start with the macroeconomic environment, narrow to a consideration of industry dynamics, and then target the specific markets in which the company competes. The criteria for the most viable strategy would then be specified, perhaps including opportunities for growth, the ability to differentiate, and the chances of a successful implementation. Next, potential strategies would be brainstormed, played off one another, and combined where appropriate.

Each strategy also needs to be evaluated in relation to how customers and competitors can be expected to respond, how the company will respond to their responses, and so on. It should also be tested against the organizational capability required to execute it. The ideal strategy may need to be amended to ensure its implementation.

Given how our minds operate and the dynamics of groups, the steps in this decision-making process should be spelled out. Posted on a flipchart, they can guide the team's thinking:

1. Define the subject of the discussion
2. Identify the key aspects of the environment affecting the issue
3. Establish the criteria to evaluate the decision
4. Brainstorm alternatives
5. Play alternatives off one another to generate more comprehensive ones
6. Evaluate the alternatives against the selection criteria

STEPS TO REWIRING

Given the benefits of participation, having a team address virtually any issue would be worthwhile. It's particularly tempting to focus on expense reduction or the obstacles hampering the performance of the business. But without first establishing the proper context for its work, a team runs the risk of creating a business that does the wrong things efficiently, or of going after symptoms rather than root causes.

It's best to approach the business strategically, working backward from a vision of the future to the actions needed to achieve it. Given the hierarchical organization of the brain, reaching agreement on the high level issues first makes it easier to make operational decisions later. The inefficiencies and obstacles will still be addressed, and the business will be poised to realize more of its potential and the team will have greater enthusiasm for its work.

Ideally, rewiring starts at the top and cascades down through the organization using the same basic process. The senior team creates a vision and a strategy for the business as a whole, but teams at lower levels also create a local vision and strategy. To ensure alignment, the team works in support of what has been formulated at the next level.

Each team begins with an analysis of the environment and then moves to a determination of customer needs and wants, competitive strengths and weaknesses (if applicable), and organizational strengths and weaknesses. All of these are analyzed relative to the others.

With this information setting the context, a vision is created, describing a point in the future when the strategy is successfully implemented and both the business and its people realize their goals. The vision statement should be short and to the point, but offer enough of the "how" to guide decision making and behavior. A strategy is then formulated to achieve the vision, leveraging the organization's strengths and minimizing its weaknesses (or turning weaknesses into strengths) to meet the needs and wants of their customers.

Implementing the strategy will usually require a series of actions that can be mapped as a flow of work through the organization. At the senior level, the activities will include identifying customer needs and wants, designing products and services, manufacturing, marketing, sales, and delivery. Supporting activities in administration, finance, and human resources, should also be addressed.

Since this is how the business would ideally operate in real time, the design of the organization should support it, ensuring a focus on the market and an efficient flow of work with minimal handoffs. But the organization should also facilitate the way people naturally work and create the kind of environment that brings out the best in people. Where possible, entrepreneurship and self-management, or at the very least participation in decision making, should be encouraged.

Making use of the way the mind works, a variety of designs are brainstormed and then tested against the appropriate criteria. The basic structure, or wiring diagram, will most likely need to be supplemented by other processes for cross-organizational communication, strategic planning, and the like. The team will also formulate a set of management practices to support the business and create the desired work environment.

It may not be possible to fully embrace the team's vision of the future, because of resource constraints or timing issues, yet even an approximation will bring improvement. But whatever the team decides is doable, a plan will be needed to manage change and it should be a narrative.

The current state of the business is the "once upon a time" beginning and the vision is the "happily ever after" end. The middle of the story is how the organization will move from where it is today to where it wants to be in the future, and it should specify what needs to change.

The final step in the process is to prioritize and sequence all of the actions formulated during the meeting, including ones for the communication of the story. The responsibility for each should be assigned to a team member, along with a due date, appropriate measures, and resource requirements. Wherever possible, the actions should be delegated to the people responsible for their implementation.

A SAMPLE AGENDA

Although the agenda for the meeting will vary from business to business, and from one level in the business to another, the broad outlines of the steps in the rewiring process and the time frames required are as follows:

DAY 1: MORNING

- Establish Behavioral Guidelines for the Team
- Structure the Decision-making Process
- Define the Business or Organizational Mission
- Analyze the Key Environmental Factors

DAY 1: AFTERNOON

- Identify Current and Future Customers' Needs and Wants
- Determine Competitors' Strengths and Weaknesses
- Assess Organizational Strengths and Weaknesses
- Draft the Vision Statement

DAY 2: MORNING

- Formulate the Strategy to Achieve the Vision
- Test the Strategy Against Customer and Competitive Responses
- Test the Strategy Against the Organization's Capability to Implement

DAY 2: AFTERNOON

- List the Activities Needed to Implement the Strategy
- Sequence and Map the Work Flow and Support Processes
- Generate Organizational Designs
- Test the Designs for Implementation and Work Environment

DAY 3: MORNING

- Formulate Supporting Management Practices
- Identify the Required Cognitive and Behavioral Changes
- Create the Organizational Narrative

DAY 3: AFTERNOON
- Review the Deliverables: Vision, Strategy, Organization, Management, and Narrative
- Formulate the Action Plan
- Assign Action Items

MAKING THE MOST OF THE EVENT

With the agenda turned into a set of questions (like "What are the customers' need and wants?"), and a watch to time discussions, a team can self-manage its rewiring process. However, there are several things that can be done to ensure the best possible result, one of which is to carefully define the manager's role during the session.

If the manager remains in control and inappropriately exercises authority, genuine participation and the free flow of ideas will stop. The manager should either assume the role of a participant and behave accordingly, or opt to only attend the end of the meeting for a final presentation of the team's recommendations.

Holding responsibility and ultimate authority, it is up to the manager to approve the team's action plan. There are three options: accept the team's recommendations, reject the team's recommendations with reasons, or take them under consideration and return with a decision within a set time frame. When this protocol is established upfront, there will be no danger of the team members feeling their work has been for naught if all of the recommendations aren't accepted.

Ideally, an external facilitator should run the meeting. Since he's not involved in the business, it's easier for him to maintain the distance needed to ensure the behavioral guidelines are adhered to and the decision-making process followed. This allows the team members to focus on their participation and removes the manager from the conflict between running the meeting and participating.

The facilitator can monitor both the interaction and the team's thought process, and when appropriate use Socratic questioning to head off any potential interpersonal conflicts and to limit unnecessary digressions. He is also responsible for ensuring that the agenda is followed and for keeping a record of the team's work.

If the facilitator is experienced in strategic planning and organizational design, he can challenge the viability of the strategy the team comes up with, and offer models for organizational design. He can also serve as a critic of the organizational narrative, making sure that it is inspirational, believable, and drives the necessary thinking and behavior.

The facilitator will be most effective if he is able to conduct interviews with all of the team members prior to their working session. These will help to build good working relationships with the team members, and to identify and resolve any interpersonal or business issues that may hamper the team's work. The information gathered will lead to the design of an agenda that addresses all of the issues team members feel are critical to the success of the business.

More often than not, the interviews will highlight the kind of disconnects that are a feature of every organization. For instance, they may reveal that the team members do not share a common vision of the business, even though they think they do, or that their relationships are not quite what they believe them to be. This dissonance can then be used to open minds and prime the team for the formulation of their behavioral guidelines.

Although using an external facilitator may require an additional expenditure upfront, it will enable the team to accomplish more in a given time frame and produce a better result. The odds are that whatever cost is involved will prove to more than worth it.

QUICK AND EFFECTIVE

Even without a facilitator and with an ample allowance for missteps, teams realize a huge return on the time they invest in rewiring the business. At the very least, the process gets everybody on the same page quickly and builds momentum for the changes that must be made to improve the business. It produces a road map to a viable and attractive future, while avoiding many of the potential pitfalls created by conventional business thinking.

Perhaps additional data will be required to support the strategic analysis. Maybe the work process may need to be mapped in greater detail. Certainly the organizational structure and systems will have to be fine-tuned. But all of this work can be undertaken after the meeting, when the organization is moving rapidly and enthusiastically forward.

When rewiring starts at the top of the organization, it focuses and aligns everyone's efforts on what's important for success. As the process moves down through the organization, employee engagement and involvement, with all of their attendant benefits, will happen as a matter of course. The senior team sets the overall direction, but the organization determines how it will be pursued.

Given the rapid changes in the environment and our proven inability to accurately forecast the future, a provisional plan, amended as more information comes in and changes are implemented, may just be best. Extensive analysis all too often leads to a plan that is obsolete by the time it's completed, but is so heavily invested in that it's difficult to change.

When rewiring the business becomes an ongoing process with brief follow-up meetings at regular intervals, the strategy and the organization are designed for flexibility from the beginning and can evolve in response to the demands of the changing environment. It's the ability to learn and change quickly that has made our species so successful in the world. The same holds true for our companies in the competitive marketplace.

NOTES

CHAPTER 1: BRAIN SCIENCE

7: **"historian of science:"** Thomas Kuhn, *The Structure of Scientific Revolutions* (Chicago: University of Chicago Press, 1996).

10–12: **"according to the neurologist:"** Antonio R. Damasio, *Descartes' Error* (New York: Picador, 1994) 212–17.

15: **"according to a person's memories:"** John J. Ratey, *A User's Guide to the Brain* (New York: Vintage, 2002) 91.

15: **"Unlike the cells:"** Number of neurons: Ratey, 9.

16: **"study of sea snail neurons:"** Eric Kandel, *In Search of Memory* (New York: Norton 2006).

17: **"supersystem of systems:"** Damasio, *Descartes' Error*, 30.

17: **"changes driven by high-level networks:"** Zindel Segal, "Brain Mapping May Guide Treatment for Depression," *Boston Globe*, Jan. 6, 2004, A 1, 13.

18: **"a patient at Memorial Sloan-Kettering:"** Michael Gazzaniga, *Human* (New York: Harper Collins, 2008) 299–300.

CHAPTER 2: FROM BRAIN TO MIND

28: **"My love:"** Robert Burns, "A Red, Red Rose," in *Eighteenth Century Poetry* (New York: Ronald Press, ed. 1956), Louis I. Bredvold, Alan D. McKillop, and Lois Whitney, 965.

29: **"the way we think:"** George Lakoff and Mark Turner, *Metaphors We Live By* (Chicago: University of Chicago Press, 2003) 3.

29: **"the source of these:"** Theodore L. Brown, *Making Truth* (Champaign: University of Illinois Press, 2003) 40.

31: **"what you see:"** Richard E. Rubenstein, *Aristotle's Children* (New York: Harcourt, 2003) 28.

32: **"our nonrandom 'designed' solutions:"** Robert Aunger, *The Electric Meme* (New York: Free Press, 2002) 220.

34: **"Story is a basic principle of mind:"** Mark Turner, *The Literary Mind* (New York: Oxford University Press, 1998) v.

35: **"Our tales are spun:"** Daniel Dennett, *Consciousness Explained* (Boston: Little, Brown, 1991) 418.

35: **"taking it as our own:"** For a fuller treatment of our identification with stories, see Michael D. Slater, "Entertainment Education and the Persuasive Impact of Narratives," in *Narrative Impact* (Mahwah, NJ: Lawrence Erlbaum, 2002) ed. Melanie C. Green, Jeffrey J. Strange, and Timothy C. Brock, 172.

36: **"the ability to read other minds:"** Jerome Bruner, *Making Stories* (Cambridge, MA: Harvard University Press, 2002) 43.

36: **"a variation of the quest masterplot:"** H. Porter Abbott, *The Cambridge Introduction to Narrative* (Cambridge, UK: Cambridge University Press, 2002) 43.

37: **"People of a particular character:"** Turner, 133.

37: **"the rogue CEO:"** Jack Hitt, "American Kabuki: The Ritual of Scandal," *New York Times*, Jul. 18, 2004.

CHAPTER 3: WORKING RELATIONSHIPS

47: **"tit for tat:"** See Robert Axelrod, *The Evolution of Cooperation* (New York: Basic Books, 1984).

48: **"One heard a news story:"** Gary Marcus, *Kluge* (Boston: Houghton Mifflin, 2008) 88.

50: **"when we speak of the 'response':"** Ervin Laszlo, *The Systems View of the World* (Cresskill, NJ: Hampton Press, 1996) 113.

54: **"mirror neurons:"** For more detail, see Gazzaniga, 100–101.

54: **"mirror neurons for emotions:"** Gazzaniga, 178–79.

54: **"theory of mind:"** Gazzaniga, 49, 261.

55: **"step into others' shoes:"** Attributed to the sales trainer, Larry Wilson.

55: **"reappraise an emotion:"** Gazzaniga, 183–84.

60: **"In the early 1980s:"** John Gabarro and John Kotter, "Managing Your Boss," *Harvard Business Review*, Jan. 8, 2008.

61: **"a scientific approach:"** See Robert Cialdini, *Influence: Science and Practice*, 4th ed. (Old Tappan, NJ: Allyn & Bacon, 2000).

CHAPTER 4: MANAGING UPSIDE DOWN

67: **"I watched, amazed:"** Jane Goodall, *Through a Window* (Boston: Houghton Mifflin, 1990) 13.

68: **"behavioral displays:"** Goodall, 43.

68: **"highly developed social skills:"** Goodall, 23.

69: **"the goal of becoming the alpha male:"** Gazzaniga, 73.

70–73: **"Frederick Winslow Taylor:"** For a complete biography, see Robert Kanigel, *The One Best Way* (Boston: Little, Brown, 1997).

72: **"cog in the machine:"** See Kanigel.

72: **"not a whit for the thinking:"** See Kanigel.

73: **"landmark study at General Electric:"** For the full study, see Herbert H. Meyer, Emmanuel Kay, and John R. P. French Jr., "Split Roles in Performance Appraisal," *Harvard Business Review*, Jan. 1, 1964.

74: **"perform boring tasks:"** Eliot Aronson, "Dissonance, Hypocrisy, and the Self-Concept," in *Cognitive Dissonance*, ed. Eddie Harmon-Jones & Judson Mills (Washington, DC: American Psychological Association, 1999) 108–9.

75: **"human beings think:"** Aronson, 107–8.

76: **"a study on reward:"** Eliot Aronson, Timothy D. Wilson, and Robin M. Akert, *Social Psychology* (Old Tappan, NJ: Prentice Hall, 2005) 147–48.

77: **"rewarding the performance:"** Aronson, et al., 147.

77: **"two groups of children:"** Aronson, et al., 181.

78: **"Unlike rats and pigeons:"** Aronson, et al., 20.

79: **"When a person's action:"** George Caspar Homans, *Social Behavior* (New York: Harcourt Brace Jovanovich, 1974) 37.

80: **"a reward he expected:"** Homans, 39.

82: **"perceived as manipulative:"** Alfie Kohn, *Punished by Rewards* (Boston: Houghton Mifflin, 1993) 119–41.

CHAPTER 5: ORGANIZING LEVERAGE

91: **"Slime mold can teach us:"** Adapted from John Bleibtreu, *The Parable of the Beast* (New York: Collier, 1968) 215–22.

93: **"the selfish gene:"** Richard Dawkins, *The Selfish Gene*, 3d ed. (New York: Oxford University Press, 2006).

93: **"Twenty-two boys were divided:"** Muzafer Sherif, *The Robbers Cave Experiment* (Middletown, CT: Wesleyan University Press, 1988).

93: **"sticks and stones:"** Judith Rich Harris, *The Nurture Assumption* (New York: Free Press, 1998) 125–27.

95: **"making pins:"** Adam Smith, *An Inquiry Into the Nature and Causes of the Wealth of Nations* (1776; 1904), www.econlib.org/LIBRARY/Smith/smWN.html, accessed Nov. 24, 2008.

96ff: **"what happened with the railroads:"** For a full discussion of the railroads, see Alfred Chandler, *The Visible Hand* (Cambridge, MA: Belknap Press, 1993).

98: **"line A or line B:"** Lauren Slater, *Opening Skinner's Box* (New York: Norton, 2004) 41.

99: **"kin selection:"** See Dawkins, 90–93, and Robert Wright, *The Moral Animal* (New York: Vintage, 1994) 156–58.

100: **"married student housing:"** For a fascinating discussion of group dynamics, see George Homans, *The Human Group* (London: Routledge & Kegan Paul, 1950).

109: **"shared stories:"** Ronald N. Jacobs, "The Narrative Integration of Personal and Collective Identity in Social Movements," in *Narrative Impact*, 206.

109: **"emphasize agency and ultimate success:"** Jacobs, 208.

109: **"a utopian future:"** Jacobs, 219.

CHAPTER 6: THINKING STRATEGICALLY

113ff: **"she must be returned:"** For the full story, see Homer, *The Iliad* (New York: Penguin, 1990), trans. Robert Fagels.

114: **"They're not thinking:"** Julian Jaynes, *The Origin of Consciousness in the Breakdown of the Bicameral Brain* (Boston: Houghton Mifflin, 1976) 60.

114ff: **"Odysseus . . . wins the war:"** For the full story of his travels, see Homer, *The Odyssey* (New York: Penguin, 1996), trans. Robert Fagels.

119: **"Sperry's research:"** For a more in-depth treatment, see Michael Gazzaniga, *The Mind's Past* (Berkeley: University of California Press, 2000).

120: **"pathologically driven:"** Marcus, 143.

121: **"torn in thought:"** Homer, *Odyssey*, Book XX, l. 7–8.

121: **"Bear up old heart:"** Homer, *Odyssey*, Book XX, l. 13.

122–24: **"Henry V's classic battle:"** For a fuller description, see Christopher Allmand, *Henry V* (Berkeley: University of California Press, 1992).

125–33: **"People Express:"** See Leonard A. Schlesinger and Debra Whitestone, "People Express (A)," (Boston: Harvard Business Publishing, 1983).

130–32: **"Stanford Marshmallow Test:"** Carey Goldberg, "Marshmallow Temptations," *Boston Globe Online*, Oct. 22, 2008, www.boston.com/news/nation/articles/2008/10/22/marshmallow_temptations_brain_scans_could_yield_vital_lessons_in_self_control/.

132: **"like a 'cloud':"** Goldberg.

132: **"Jeremy Gray:"** Goldberg.

CHAPTER 7: CHANGING MINDS

139–41: **"drive a dolphin crazy:"** Morris Berman, *The Reenchantment of the World* (Ithaca, NY: Cornell University Press, 1984) 229–30.

142: **"reversals of logic:"** Arthur Koestler, *The Act of Creation* (1967) 65.

148: **"generate opposite results:"** Jamshid Gharajedaghi, *Systems Thinking* (Burlington, MA: Elsevier, 1999) 48.

150: **"processing novel information:"** Elkhonon Goldberg, *The Executive Brain* (New York: Oxford University Press, 2001) 43.

151: **"cognitive restructuring:"** Michael R. Leippe and Donna Eisenstadt, "A Self-Accountability Model of Dissonance Reduction," in *Cognitive Dissonance*, 204.

152: **"embedded in a large network:"** Leippe and Eisenstadt, 205.

152: **"a growing number of law enforcement professionals:"** Johann Hari, "What Will the Candidates Do to End the Unwinnable War on Drugs? *Huffington Post*, Aug. 13, 2008, www.huffingtonpost.com/johann-hari/what-will-the-candidates_b_118045.html, accessed Nov. 24, 2008.

153: **"two different types of change:"** Paul Watzlawick, John Weakland, and Richard Fisch, *Change* (1974), 10–11.

154: **"a couple on a sailboat:"** Watzlawick, et al., 37.

155: **"overly dependent children:"** Watzlawick, et al., 116–19.

155: **"emotional setting or viewpoint:"** Watzlawick, et al., 95.

158: **"expectation gone awry:"** Bruner, 28.

158: **"peripeteia:"** Aristotle, *Introduction to Aristotle*, ed. Richard McKeon (New York: Modern Library, 1992) 679.

159: **"some sort of resolution:"** Bruner, 16–17.

CHAPTER 8: LEADING IDEAS

165: **"we think of these as 'multiple drafts':**" Dennett, 113.

165: **"narrative stream:"** Dennett, 113.

167: **"the movie *Patton*:"** *Patton* (Twentieth Century Fox, 1970).

168: **"authoritarian leadership:"** Bernard M. Bass, *Bass & Stogdill's Handbook of Leadership* (New York: Free Press, 1990) 442.

170: **"pay-for-performance:"** Bass, 362.

170: **"repetitive, boring, and tedious:"** Bass, 364.

170: **"the manager's reasons:"** Bass, 365.

171: **"definitions of leadership:"** Jay A. Conger, *Learning to Lead* (San Francisco: Jossey-Bass, 1992) 18.

171: **"360-degree feedback:"** Bass, 514.

172: **"'transactional' and 'transformational':"** James McGregor Burns, *Leadership* (New York: Harper Collins, 1978).

172: **"transformational leaders consistently outperform:"** Bass, 525.

172: **"supplement transactional leadership:"** Bass, 525.

173–75: **"Henry's response":** All quotes from *Shakespeare: The Complete Works*, ed. G.B. Harrison (1968).

176: **"what ... transformational leaders do:"** Bass, 184–221.

177: **"studies demonstrating ... participation:"** Bass, 436–71.

177: **"less participative:"** Bass, 441.

179: **"create ... rather than record:"** Joseph LeDoux, *Synaptic Self* (New York: Viking Penguin, 2002) 319.

179: **"A college class:"** Aronson, et al., 62.

179: **"bloomers:"** Aronson, et al., 70.

180: **"the performance of salespeople:"** J. Sterling Livingston, "The Pygmalion Effect," *Harvard Business Review*, Jan. 1, 2006.

180: **"a seminal article:"** Abraham Zaleznik, "Managers and Leaders: Are They Different?" *Harvard Business Review*, Jan. 1, 2004.

184: **"expectation ... charismatic:"** Bass, 197.

CHAPTER 9: ALL THINGS ARE READY

195: **"civilization's greatest economic powers:"** See David Landes, *The Wealth and Poverty of Nations* (New York: Norton, 1998) 213–23.

201: **"the sheer sake of doing it:"** Mihály Csikszentmihályi, *Flow* (New York: Harper Collins, 1990) 4.

201: **"forget everything else:"** Csikszentmihályi, 6.

202: **"you must love your work:"** George Eliot, *Middlemarch* (1872; 1965) 606.

ACKNOWLEDGMENTS

The ideas in this book just build on our three-thousand-year-old tradition of speculating on how the mind works and how best to use it. But in the twenty-first century, we have an advantage: the *f*MRI that enables us to actually see the brain at work. Scientists Stephen Pinker, Antonio Damasio, Michael Gazzaniga, and others have taken the discoveries of neuroscience and demonstrated what they mean for the way we live. My work would not have been possible without their insights.

Nor would it have been possible without the clients who have invited me into their companies and allowed me to be part of their efforts to transform their businesses. I know that I've learned at least as much from them as they've learned from me. In particular, I'm indebted to my client and friend Ben Levitan. He's become my barometer on trends in the business world and a sure-fire connection to anybody anywhere. His help and encouragement have been invaluable.

I've also been fortunate to have as my agents Kristina and

Michael of the Ebeling Agency. They embody the heart of the new approach to business that I present in this book. They challenged accepted practice and rewrote the rules of author representation to place my book with a great publisher in record time. They have continued to provide much needed counsel and advice.

But my greatest debt is to my editor, Courtney Young. She took my ideas and taught me how to make what might have been a difficult subject easily accessible. The packaging of the book, its structure, and the clarity of the writing are all due to her efforts. While she set challenging expectations, she was always first and foremost a true partner in the work. Without her, there wouldn't be a *Management Rewired*. And without the diligent efforts of my publicist at Portfolio, Courtney Nobile, probably nobody would even know about the book. My thanks to a great team.

INDEX